The *Real* Naked Truth

Good Success God's Way
Lifetime Guarantee

Kent Mattox

Real: Not artificial, fraudulent, or illusory: genuine—being precisely what the name implies.
Naked: Devoid of concealment or disguise.
Truth: Sincerity in action, character, and utterance.

The Real Naked Truth, by author Kent Mattox, is a paradigm shifting look at enjoying a successful life based on Kingdom principles while living in the world system. The introductory paragraph sets us up for fresh insight into what good success really looks like, "Let's face it; everyone wants to be a success. However, there is a difference between success and *good* success. *Good* success is the kind of success that comes from God and is significant. Contrary to popular belief, God wants His people to be successful."

The *Real* Naked Truth

**Real: Not artificial, fraudulent, or illusory: genuine—being
precisely what the name implies.
Naked: Devoid of concealment or disguise.
Truth: Sincerity in action, character, and utterance**

Chapter One

L et's face it; everyone wants to be a success. However, there is
a difference between success and *good* success. *Good* success
is the kind of success that comes from God and is significant.
Contrary to popular belief, God wants His people to be successful.
Religious traditions have convinced many believers that God does not
want us to succeed. When you really think about that as theology or even
theory, it makes absolutely no sense whatsoever. When we fail or do not
become successful at what God has called us to do, He receives no honor
from our failures. There is no celebration in failed marriages, lack of
education, not paying our bills, or being sick. God can take all of those
circumstances and turn them around for our good but it is not, and has
never been, His plan for us to live defeated lives. He is glorified when He
takes a situation and turns it into a success, but His ultimate plan is for us
to experience triumph without tragedy.

The key is to know and understand the Word of God for ourselves
and not count on someone else's revelation or interpretation of God's
Word. Hence the real naked truth is that God does want us to prosper.

God really wants us to prosper in every area of our lives. I
have read the Bible from Genesis to Revelation and I have come to
this conclusion—God's desire to deliver us is greater than the devil's
desire to destroy us. God is loving, merciful, and wants us to succeed
at everything that we do when it is according to His plan, purpose, and
destiny for our lives. God *really* wants us to succeed.

Traditional beliefs and religion have blinded God's people and
kept them from living a life of good success. Matthew 15:6 tells us this,
"whoever says to his father or mother, 'Whatever profit you might have
received from me is a gift to God,' then he need not honor his father

or mother. Thus you have made the commandment of God of no effect by your tradition." God does want us to live a lifetime full of success and He guarantees us that if we are obedient to His Word and avoid vain philosophies as Colossians 2: 8 encourages to do, "Beware lest anyone cheat you through philosophy and empty deceit, according to the tradition of men, according to the basic principles of the world, and not according to Christ," we will learn to be successful in God and live a very blessed, prosperous life.

Ephesians 1: 15-18 is Paul's prayer for the Galatians, "I pray that the eyes of their understanding would be opened and that the truth of God's Word would be illuminated and revealed to them, ... that the Father of glory, may give to you the spirit of wisdom and revelation in the knowledge of Him, the eyes of your understanding being enlightened; that you may know what is the hope of His calling, what are the riches of the glory of His inheritance in the saints…"

We all have traditions that have become part of our human experience. All of our traditional, holiday festivities that so many of us cherish have their beginnings somewhere. Recently we did a little research to find out where Thanksgiving, Christmas and wedding traditions have their origins. One of my favorite stories is the one of a new to the family daughter-in-law who wanted to know the reason her husband's sisters cut the ends off of their holiday hams. She called each one and the answers varied. One said it was because it made the ham juicer. Another said it was because the ham browned more evenly. The third said she didn't have a clue but she would call her mom and get back to her. The very next day she did call back and told her new sister-in-law the reason her mom cut the ends off of the ham was because when she was first married they could not afford to buy a pan big enough for the ham so she cut the ends off. A tradition was born. Too often it is our nature to not ask questions but rather to continue to do what we have seen or heard others do.

Once again, the key for us, as believers, is *to understand* that we have a very real adversary and that we are in a spiritual war. We have to contend earnestly for our faith just as Jude 1:3 admonishes us to do, "Beloved, while I was very diligent to write to you concerning our common salvation, I found it necessary to write to you exhorting you to contend earnestly for the faith which was once for all delivered to the saints." 2 Corinthians 4:4 lays out one the enemies' most effective strategies, "But if our gospel be hid, it is hid to them that are lost: In whom the god of this world has blinded the minds of them which believe not, lest the light of the glorious gospel of Christ, who is the image of God, should shine unto them."

In Matthew 23: 27 Jesus taught very strongly about having faith in God versus living a life dictated by men's traditions and religious rites and ceremonies, "Woe to you, scribes and Pharisees, hypocrites. For you are like whitewashed tombs which indeed appear beautiful outwardly, but inside are full of dead men's bones and all uncleanness."

Mark 11: 12, and 19-25 is a great object lessons for all of us, "Now the next day, when they had come out from Bethany, He was hungry. And seeing from afar a fig tree having leaves, He went to see if perhaps He would find something on it. When He came to it, He found nothing but leaves, for it was not the season for figs. In response Jesus said to it, "Let no one eat fruit from you ever again." And His disciples heard it. When evening had come, He went out of the city. Now in the morning, as they passed by, they saw the fig tree dried up from the roots. And Peter, remembering, said to Him, "Rabbi, look the fig tree which You cursed has withered away." So Jesus answered and said to them, "Have faith in God. For assuredly, I say to you, whoever says to this mountain, 'Be removed and be cast into the sea,' and does not doubt in his heart, but believes that those things he says will be done, he will have whatever he says. Therefore I say to you, whatever things you ask when you pray, believe that you receive them, and you will have them."

Jesus used the fig tree as an illustration to teach the disciples, and us, to have faith in God, not man or vain philosophies. Throughout the Word trees represent success and prosperity. Isaiah 61:3 declares this, "To appoint unto them that mourn in Zion, ...that they might be called trees of righteousness, the planting of the Lord, that He might be glorified. Psalm 1: 1-3 describes the process as we grow into successful, prosperous people, "Blessed is the man that walks not in the counsel of the ungodly, nor stands in the way of sinners, nor sits in the seat of the scornful. But his delight is in the law of the Lord; and in His law does he meditate day and night. And he shall be like a tree planted by the rivers of water, that brings forth his fruit in his season, his leaf also shall not wither; and whatsoever he does shall prosper."

Allegorical trees and object lessons are for our admonition and understanding. Adam and Eve may represent the greatest life lesson we can learn from trees in Genesis 2:25. When given the choice between the Tree of Life and the Tree of the Knowledge of Good and Evil the world's first couple went from, "they were both naked, the man and his wife, and were not ashamed," to, Genesis 3:7 when "the eyes of both of them were opened, and they knew that they were naked; and they sewed fig leaves (man-made religion) together and made themselves coverings."

God's plan is for us to live life filled with good success. Proverbs chapter three illuminates the real naked truth of God's plan *and* gives us clear direction to not only obtain good success but to live it.

Whatever State of Mind, Be Content

Psalm 1:1-3 tells us, "Blessed is the man who walks not in the council of the ungodly, nor stands in the path of sinners, nor sits in the seat of the scornful but his delight is in the law of the Lord and in His law does he meditate day and night. He shall be like a tree planted by the rivers of water that brings forth fruit in its season whose leaf shall not wither and whatsoever he does shall prosper."

He wants us to be like trees that are immovable. Trees are not easily shaken; they are not easily moved when the wind blows and they have deep roots. The Word is speaking directly of our faith and trust in our heavenly Father in this portion of Scripture, "He shall be like trees... planted by a river of water so that even in dry times your leaf will not wither, you will just keep on bearing fruit." God's design is that we become trees planted by the River of Life.

True seekers of Christ are attracted to a particular church. In those churches there are people who enjoy the Fruits of the Spirit. We all have spiritual gifts, and when all of these gifts are flowing together, an atmosphere of mercy and grace begins to produce spiritual fruit that is pleasing to God. That is what success looks like to our heavenly Father.

People will come far and wide to experience an environment where the Fruit of the Spirit is being demonstrated. The Fruit of the Spirit is peace, joy, love, gentleness, kindness, meekness, generosity, and faith. The only two we are to enjoy personally are peace and joy. The others are for the people around us. If we do not have a lot of people seeking us out, we need to check our fruit.

As we grow in our gifts and begin to demonstrate more of the Fruit of the Holy Spirit, it is important to take into consideration who we are in relationship with. We are not to walk in the counsel of the ungodly, nor stand in the path of sinners or sit in the seat of the scornful. Whoever we fellowship with will ultimately become a determining factor in our success. We cannot be in relationship with negative people or those who have "stinking thinking." I do not like to be around people who are always trying to discourage me.

I like to be around people who encourage me and who will lift me up, not pull me down. We must choose to be in relationship with positive, content people who will encourage us. It is useless to tell anybody your problems. Statistically, 90% of people do not care about our problems and the other 10% are glad we have them. Why even voice the negative aspects of our lives? Paul said to think on these things, things that are edifying, exhortative, and glorifying to God.

It should be a very specific strategy on our part to seek to spend time and build relationships with people who know who they are in Christ. Often I arrive at church weak, wasted, and in want, but when I leave I am encouraged, exhorted, and edified. I may be down and depressed but before I know it, I have the peace of God. Why is that? It is because I place myself in the position to be around the Fruit of the Spirit growing in mature believers and soon I am enjoying joy, mercy, grace, kindness, and love. I may have arrived hungry but I leave full. I choose to seek out His people who are full of the Spirit of God and who are trees planted by the River of Life.

Why Does God Want Me to Prosper?

Religion would make us think we are already trees of life, producing the Fruit of the Spirit when in fact, we are not. Mark 11:12 describes fruitless religion perfectly, "Now the next day when Jesus had come out of Bethany, He was hungry and seeing from afar a fig tree having leaves, He went to see perhaps if He would find something on it. When He came to it He found nothing but leaves, for it was not yet the season for figs. In response, Jesus said to it 'let no one eat fruit from you again,' and His disciples heard it."

The first few times I read that I wondered if Jesus was having bad day. It simply did not make sense to me that Jesus would pass by a tree that had no fruit on it and curse it. The way I saw it He was hungry, there was no fruit on the tree, and He cursed it because there was nothing for Him to eat. I thought Jesus must have gotten up on the wrong side of the bed that morning or perhaps the disciples had angered Him. Of course, I realized that could not be the case because Jesus did not behave that way. He was the Son of God, so we know it was not because He was having a bad day. We have bad days and behave inappropriately but Jesus is the same yesterday, today, and forever.

The Word explains that it was not even the season for figs, so I wondered why Jesus would curse a tree knowing it was not even the season for them to be there. So what is this Scripture actually meant to teach us? The parable begins as Jesus, Who is hungry, begins to look for fruit. It was a mature tree that was supposed to have fruit on it. When He came upon the fig tree, there were only leaves. Because it was not yet the season for figs means it was not yet the season for the figs to be harvested. There are only two times you will find leaves on a fig tree, either with the fruit or after the fruit. However, you will never find fruit before there are leaves. If there are leaves on a fig tree, there should be fruit on the tree unless it has been harvested.

When Jesus saw leaves, He was truly expecting there to be figs to eat. As He got closer to the tree, He saw there were leaves but no fruit, and He cursed it. This was not done in anger but rather was an object lesson for the disciples. He left the tree without fruit and went directly to the temple where they were selling and trading things. The money changers really angered Him, and He whipped them out of the temple. Contrary to popular belief, it was not because they were selling pilgrims doves and the like for their sacrifices. In the Jewish culture, sacrifices were purchased because it was required that everyone have a sacrifice when they came into the temple. Jesus was so angry because they were shortchanging people. They were selling cheap merchandise for a high price.

Jerusalem was a challenge for many of the farmers and country people who came to worship. It would be like my first time traveling internationally. On my first trip to Rome, I went to the Sistine Chapel. I was awestruck by how beautiful it was. After the amazing experience of seeing the incredible artwork by renowned artists, I called my wife. I excitedly began to share everything I had just seen. I said, "You won't believe this but I am in this chapel and there are paintings on the ceiling, on the walls, and on the floor. It is called the 16th Chapel." She said, "Honey, I believe that is the Sistine Chapel." I said, "No, no, there are many of them and this is the 16th one." She said, "Honey, I'm sure it's the Sistine." I asked, "Who is in Rome, you or me?" Because she loves me she didn't debate the issue, and I continued to make a fool of myself as I persisted in telling everybody it was the 16th Chapel until finally somebody I would listen to corrected me. I was exactly like the country folks that came to Jerusalem for the first time. We can only imagine how innocent villagers visiting the city were taken advantage of by their more cunning and sophisticated city dwelling counterparts.

They were getting shortchanged and it really hacked Jesus off. So He whipped the money changers out of the temple saying, "You cannot treat My people like this. You have turned My Father's house into a den of thieves." It made sense when I read it in context. The fig leaves represented something far more insidious than there just being no fruit on the tree. What did Adam and Eve try to cover themselves with? They tried to hide their nakedness with fig leaves. In this parable, Jesus teaches His disciples that fig leaves speak of man-made religion.

Religion and tradition that represent the barrenness of man's soul will never satisfy, will never cause us to prosper, and will cause us to *not* succeed in the things of God. Actually, man-made religion will shortchange us. We will arrive hungry and leave unsatisfied. That is the naked truth.

Just Have Faith

If our faith is based in an association, denomination, or organization, or if we have put faith in man and not God, it is cursed. Jeremiah 17:5 states, "He that trusts in man is cursed but he that trusts in God is blessed." If we place our faith anywhere but in God, we are not going to be successful. Men will fail us every time but God never will.

That is why at the end of this story Peter said, "The tree you cursed is dead, it happened just as You said." Jesus responded with, "Just have faith in God." Never trust man-made religion. Never trust things that look like they have fruit but do not. Religion looks like fruit but there is no substance and provides nothing nutritional. Religion says the right things and wears the right clothes, but it is a white-washed sepulcher where we will find counterfeit goods. He does not want us to be like that. He wants us to produce fruit and multiply. God does not look at the outside, He looks at the inside, and it is His plan that we have something to feed people.

To produce anything for the Kingdom of God we first have to be planted. Psalm 92:13 states, "Those who are planted in the House of the Lord shall flourish in the courts of their God." If we are going to be trees by rivers of water, we are going to have to be planted. We have to allow our lives to be sown into the soil God put us in and we have to stay there.

The adversary of our soul, also known as the devil, will cause offenses to come by hurt feelings, disappointment, rejection, misunderstandings, and a multitude of other emotions that we are all susceptible to. Because of the redemptive Blood of Jesus Christ, the enemy can no longer accuse us before the throne of God. However, he can create enough havoc that we begin to accuse one another. His ultimate goal is to pit believers against one another so that offense comes from someone that we trust and respect and who is usually the least likely candidate for disappointing behavior to come from.

Offenses will come in every scenario you could imagine and in just as many varieties of relationships. One of the most insidious being the way it seeps into church via a perceived or real offense by a pastor or someone in leadership. Once that breach has turned into a misunderstanding that neither party is willing to have restored, the enemy has us right where he wants us. One or the other party begins to disassociate and pull up roots. The river that once provided life has now been polluted by human actions and reactions, and the once life-giving flow has been poisoned by unforgiveness, anger, and bitterness.

If Satan can get us to pull our roots up enough times, our roots will die and we may never prosper in God. We will run from church to church, or worse leave our faith altogether, never being properly planted long enough to grow strong roots. When God leads us to make a move, it takes place in a completely different manner. We are sent out and blessed as we go. That type of change is usually a promotion in the Kingdom and a call answered in obedience.

God and man honor obedience, but honor does not come when we are uprooted because of an offense. Why doesn't God honor uprooting ourselves out of anger? It is because we take the same hurts and wounds we have with us and the same cycle of being planted, then uprooted, begins all over again. We will never be completely healed until we plant ourselves and say, "I am not going any further until I am healed and my purpose is fulfilled."

The Bible is clear on this subject in Psalm 119:165, "Those who love the Word, nothing by any means offends them." We have to stay planted where God has sent us. We have to be purposed and make the choice that we are not going to allow offenses or misunderstandings to be the reason that we are uprooted from the place God has planted us. When we plant a seed, we do not see the plant or the harvest overnight. Jesus admonished the disciples about this very issue by pointing out their lack of faith. He is not talking about an amount or measure of faith. He is talking about a time-line, our duration of faith. According to the Word, it only takes the faith of a grain of mustard seed to produce something, so it is not about measure or size. He is talking about time. When Jesus said, "You of little faith," He was talking about those who waited only a *little time*.

We get so impatient that when we are planted we want to see the fruit or the harvest immediately. However, God does not do things the way we think they should be done. God plants us then there is a season that we are literally going through the metamorphosis of changing from seedling to plant. During the gestation period, we cannot see the growth because our roots are being established and must go down deeply before the first signs of life appear on the surface. We can grow a squash in two months, but it takes a hundred years to grow an oak tree. God is not interested in us becoming squash but He is interested in us developing into strong trees with deep roots. It may take a while for the seed to take root and for fruit to develop, but when we allow Him to do the work and continue in well doing, we will prosper if we faint not. We are all in a time of waiting, so be encouraged. It is not time to pull up our roots, it is time to plant ourselves and purpose in our hearts that we will not be moved from the position God has placed us in. The harvest is coming and we were planted for such a time as this.

Luke 13:6-9 tells us, "He spoke a parable to a certain man who had a fig tree planted in his vineyard and came seeking fruit but found none. He said to the keeper of the vineyard, 'Look, I have come for three years seeking fruit on this fig tree, and found none. Cut it down. Why does it use up the ground?'" Do you know Who is asking that question? The answer is Jesus. You may ask how I know that. Well, the answer to that is it is written in the Bible in red. Jesus said, "It is taking up ground." Jesus had grown weary of people taking up ground and not bearing any fruit. Jesus said this and the steward answered him, "Sir, let it alone this year until I dig around it and fertilize it."

Endure the Manure

If we are going to bear fruit and have good success, we are going to get fertilized. What do you fertilize things with? The answer, simply put, is manure. In Christian terms we can say it this way, manure happens. If we can learn to endure manure and know that there is going to be a fertilization process, we are more than halfway there.

I have had some manure (fertilization) in my life. How about you? Why does it have to happen that way? The answer is things happen. Of course, no one has all the answers why, but things do happen for a purpose. If we allow these things (trying times, trauma, tragedy) to fertilize us, we will begin to grow. If we can endure the smell for a while and allow God to fertilize our lives, we will bear a lot of fruit for the Kingdom. Have you ever driven past a field just after it has been fertilized? The smell will just about knock you out. However, when you drive by a few weeks later, the air has been cleansed by the passage of time, the fertilizer has done its work, and the field is starting to yield its crop. Why? The answer is this: the greater the concentration of the manure, the greater value the fertilizer, and the bigger the harvest will be. The good news for us is the more manure we have endured, the bigger the harvest we are going to have in our lives. Endure the manure, and great will be your reward.

Planted, Fertilized, and Pruned

Planted, fertilized, and pruned—does that describe you? John 15:1-2 states, "I am the true vine and My Father is the vine dresser. Every branch of Me that does not bear fruit He takes away; but every branch that bears fruit He prunes, that it may bear more fruit." There will be a time when God will start cutting distractions out of our lives. He will prune anything that is not producing something of value for the Kingdom. It may be in our relationships. We may not understand why an association has ended, but God does because He has the master plan for our lives. Some relationships are for a lifetime; however, some are for just a season. Oftentimes, God removes us from familiar relationships because He is taking us to an unfamiliar place that we have been prepared for and our contemporaries have not.

When relationships change, it is not a time to question God's direction for our lives. The key is to know the Word of God and to walk with Him daily, listening for the small, still voice of the Holy Spirit to encourage, equip, and enable us to see beyond the present circumstance to the greater purpose. When we are familiar with the seasons that God has for us, they do not come as such a surprise. Remember, God's plan is for our good and His glory. God has no desire to see us broken and beaten by what we perceive as failures when, in fact, He has allowed change to happen so we can be the most effective witnesses that we can be for His will to be accomplished.

God always sees His promise and future purpose for us while we tend, as human beings, to dwell on our present problems. We must learn to embrace the different seasons in our lives. The pruning process, much like the fertilization process, is not always the most pleasant aspect of our Christian commitment, especially if we have been through trial after trial, do not know the Word of God, do not fellowship with Jesus, and keep going around the same mountain of problems over and over again. It is time to wake up. God has done everything to prepare, propel, and propitiate us into His plans and purposes. It is time to embrace the process and mature into the productive believer God designed us to be.

God prunes old things out of our lives that are not producing life and reproducing Him. Have you ever seen bushes that gardeners cut back? The branches look naked and exposed yet when it is their season, they grow back fuller than ever before producing more foliage and fruit than the previous season of growth. When we go through times of feeling as though we are naked and exposed, God is cutting back our branches to the point where there is new life. It is a painful process but He is getting us ready to be more productive.

Be encouraged. If you have been planted but have not yet seen a lot of fruit, just hang on, because the deeper your roots, the greater the yield. If you have had to endure manure and have had to be fertilized for a while, endure because God is going to bring you out of those circumstances. All the trials you have been through will produce more for the Kingdom of God than you could have ever imagined.

If you have been through the pruning process, it certainly was not because God did not want you to succeed. It is because He is getting you ready for the next level of increase. God gave me a prophetic word about this very issue. Philippians 4:11-13 states, "Not that I speak in regard to need, for I learned in whatever state I am in, to be content. I know how to be abased, and I know how to abound. Everywhere and in all things I have learned to be full and to be hungry, both to abound and to suffer need. I can do all things through Christ who strengthens me."

Some who will read this have learned to be abased. They have learned how to do with little. They have learned how to walk in difficult circumstances and they have learned how to walk through trials. Moreover, they have learned how to be content in bad situations. By knowing His Word, a place of contentment has been found that can only be found in Him.

Being successful means that whatever state we are in, whether we are in or out of trials, whether we have a lot or a little, whether everything is going well or everything is falling apart, we are content knowing that God is going to produce good success in our lives. Many people in church right now have been in a season of learning how to be abased. The Body is learning that we can do all things through Christ who strengthens us when we are doing what He has called us to do. There have been times in my life that I have had to learn how to do without things and learn to be content, but even then I knew that it was not something I had accomplished in my own strength. It was supernatural strength that kept me strong.

When we submit our lives to God, He will teach us how to be abased and content. Then there will come a day when He will teach us how to abound and remain humble. He that humbles himself shall be exalted. If you have been through a season of learning how to be abased, get ready, God promises He will teach us to abound. Just as we had the strength to be abased, we will now have the strength, with humility, to abound.

God is not a man that He would lie and He keeps His promises. We must believe that He is God and rewards those who diligently seek Him. If we walk through life expecting God to do good things for us and do not let religious traditions lie and cheat us out of what God has for us, the Word promises we will become successful in life.

15

Every one of our needs will be supplied according to His riches in glory *and* we will have abundance so we can meet someone else's needs. Joy, fearless living, happiness, and peace—that is good success and God wants us to live it.

Jeremiah 29:11 reminds us, "For I know the plans I have for you says God, plans to succeed and to give you a good and expected end." God sees us somewhere in the future and we look a lot better than we do right now. Sometimes we have to lose our perception of success to actually experience it God's way. Jesus said in Matthew 10:39, "If you will lose your life, you will find it but if you try to save it, you will lose it." God's desire is for us to surrender everything to Him and let Him take control of our lives. Through that surrender we will begin to enjoy Good Success.

God *IS* Great

Great: Remarkable in magnitude, degree, or effectiveness.

Chapter Two

Upon entering the Promised Land, as Joshua stepped into Moses' big shoes, Joshua 1: 7-9 makes God's intentions clear for the new commander in chief, "I will give you good success." We have learned from the Word of God that it is God's will for us to succeed in life and that the blessing of the Lord makes one successful and adds no sorrow with it. God's plan is for us to live successful lives as believers spiritually, physically, emotionally, financially, and in every area of our lives. The formula that we need for a successful life is found in Proverbs 3:1-14:

"My son do not forget my law, but let your heart keep my commands. For length of days, and long life and peace they will add to you. Let not mercy and truth forsake you. Bind them around your neck, write them on the tablet of your heart, and so find favor and high esteem in the sight of God and man. Trust in the Lord with all your heart, and lean not unto your own understanding. In all your ways acknowledge Him, and He shall direct your paths. Do not be wise in your own eyes. Fear the Lord, depart from evil. It will be health to your flesh, strength to your bones. Honor the Lord with your possessions in the first fruits of all your increase, so your barns will be filled with plenty, and your vats will overflow with new wine. Do not despise the chastening of the Lord, nor detest His correction. For, whom the Lord loves, He corrects, even as the Father, the Son, in whom He delights. Happy is the man who finds wisdom, and the man who gains understanding, for its proceeds are better than the profits of silver, and her gain than fine gold."

In this portion of Scripture, every command comes with a blessing. *If you will* not forget My law, you will have length of days, long life, and peace. *If you will* be merciful, you will walk in truth and have favor and high esteem. *If you will* trust in the Lord, He will direct your paths. *If you will* fear the Lord and depart from evil, it will be health to your flesh and strength to your bones. *If you will* honor the Lord with your possessions and the first fruits of all your increase, your barns will be filled with plenty and your vats will overflow with new wine. *If you will* find wisdom, you will be happy. Every command that God gives comes with a blessing.

The first Scripture is clearly about obedience: "My son, do not forget My law, but let your heart keep My commands, for length of days, and long life, and peace they will add to you." Dr. Paul Yongi Cho (a Korean pastor of one of the largest churches in the world with over one million people in attendance) was asked, "What is the key to your success?" His reply was very simple. "I pray and obey." When we walk in obedience to God, we will enjoy good success. We, as the Body of Christ, need to realize our perception of God has been perverted. God is not in heaven making lists of commands, waiting to beat us over the head if we do not keep them. That is not what the commands of God are about.

Obedience is for Our Benefit

Obedience is for our benefit. God does not need anything. It does not change God when we are obedient. God is God. The reason God wants us to obey is for our benefit. God gives us a reason to obey because there is an end result that benefits us. The church has had the wrong impression of God's intentions. We think we are God's slaves on earth and He is making demands, and if we do not adhere to them then we are going to be punished by a vengeful God. The fear of the Lord is reverential, but it is the love of God that draws us to Him. We are His sons and daughters, not slaves. Most of us live our lives without real success because we never have real peace in our relationship with our Creator.

I John 4:18 tells us, "Perfect love casts out all fear." God is Love, not fear. To be fearful of God is not to be afraid that He is going to kill you. To fear God is to reverence and worship Him. I serve God because He is so good to me, not because He treats me badly. Proverbs 3:1 starts out with these two words: *My son* and that denotes one thing, relationship. God does not want us to serve as slaves. He wants us to serve Him because of our relationship as sons and daughters. Obedience comes as the result of our relationship.

Hebrews 5:10 reads, "Jesus, though He was a Son, learned obedience by the things which He suffered." We learn obedience to God by the things we suffer, or to put it plainly, by the trials and circumstances that God *brings us through*. Jesus suffered, *obeying* God, not *disobeying* God. Sometimes, as sons of God, we suffer because our obedience oftentimes brings persecution.

Obeying God causes us to walk a different path than those who live in the world system. It may be a hard road for a while, but at the end we will find God's blessings. Mark 10: 29-30 exhorts us to understand what Jesus promises us, "So Jesus answered and said, 'Assuredly, I say to you, there is no one who has left house or brothers or sisters or father or mother or wife or children or lands, for My sake and the gospel's, who shall not receive a hundredfold now in this time, houses and brothers and sisters and mothers and children and lands, with persecutions, and in the age to come, eternal life.'" Sometimes we suffer because of the consequences of disobedience. However, as we choose to live our lives by godly principles, we are going to be successful in Him. It is imperative that we realize our perception of God—as an unjust judge waiting to smite us every time we make a mistake is perverted. If we suffer for obedience or disobedience, we suffer as sons.

Lookin' Good

This misperception of God is as ridiculous as a photo that I found of myself recently. In this photo I am in the eighth grade, and as I viewed it I tried to remember what I could have possibly been thinking as I got dressed that day. Those long ago thoughts are a revelation. It reminds me of that country song that has the chorus: *I know what I was feeling, but what was I thinking?* I thought I looked great and to this day can still evoke those memories and relive the era and the times of the 70's.

In this photographic moment, I obviously believe I am lookin' good! My hair is long, I haven't quite hit my growth spurt yet, and I am built a bit like a truck. Unfortunately, I had chosen the height of fashion of the day and dressed myself in a lime green*, polyester* suit. To add injury to insult, I am wearing platform shoes! To quote another country song, *man did I look cheesy!* I understand why the 70's are considered to be the lost decade concerning everything from politics to fashion. Thankfully, many things have changed since then in our nation, so why hasn't the church? My point is the view that we have of God waiting for us to fail so He can punish us falls firmly into the category of what the heck have we been thinking for these thousands of years?

For those of us who have children, we know that just because they do not make their beds or clean their rooms that we are not going to curse them with sickness because they did not obey us. They are our sons and daughters. We may discipline them or put them on restriction, but we are not going to do something that might destroy their lives. Unfortunately, so many of us have been taught that if we are not obedient then God is going to punish us by allowing poverty or infirmity to attack our lives.

Genesis chapters one and two lay out God's plan for Adam. God

19

created Adam to fellowship with Him. Adam disobeyed God, but that did not change God. However, it did change Adam. God was still the same. God asked, "Adam, where are you?" God was still looking for fellowship and relationship, but because Adam had disobeyed, his own heart condemned him. So what happens when we disobey God? It does not change God's love for us, but it does change our feelings toward Him.

I John 3:20-22 states: "If our heart condemns us, God is greater than our heart. If our heart does not condemn us, we have confidence toward God, and whatsoever we ask, we shall receive." Realistically, the reason prayers are not answered is because we have not asked the right questions or we have disobeyed God, and condemned our own hearts, so when we come to God, we do not come in faith. We come asking, "God, how in the world can You bless me since I have been disobedient?" Truthfully, it is really way past time to understand once and for all that obeying God is not about God changing His heart towards *us*, it is about us changing our hearts towards *Him*. When we know we have obeyed God, we have a clear conscience and great faith that we are asking correctly, living in His will and expecting Him to answer clearly. As we obey and walk by faith, we will begin to enjoy good success.

God Does Chasten Those He Loves

God will, at times, chasten us for not listening to His direction but it is always for our profit. Hebrews 12:6 reminds us that God will chasten us as sons. On the one hand, we have to understand that the two commandments we were left by Jesus are literally to love God with all our hearts and to love our neighbor as ourselves. On the other hand, we have to look at the fact that church and religion put a lot of demands on people that have nothing to do with loving God or our neighbors. Like the Pharisees we lay heavy burdens on the people and do not even lift a finger to remove them. That is not God's plan for us. The Israelites started with Ten Commandments but by the time man was through adding to them, they had grown into seven hundred and ninety. Jesus reduced those to the two most important to our heavenly Father. In Luke 10: 27 He said, "Love God with all your heart, your soul, and your mind, and love your neighbor as yourself."

When we love God with all of our heart and our neighbor as ourselves, we are keeping all the commandments and His commandments are not grievous. I John 5:3 reminds us, "His commands are not burdensome." That is why in Matthew 11:30 Jesus says, "Come unto Me, all you that labor and are heavy laden. Learn of Me, take My yoke upon you, for My yoke is easy and My burden is light." Lamentations 3:33 tells us, "For God does not afflict the children willfully, nor grieve the children of men." It is not God's plan to load us down with burdensome commandments. He wants us to succeed in life as we are obedient to His Word.

When we diligently seek His will for our lives, He will instruct us in a very personal way. That is why it is important to hear and obey God. He has different walks and different plans for each of us. Other than those two commands, God's instructions are custom designed to suit each calling and gift that He has given to us.

I Corinthians 12: 7-10 explains to us that spiritual gifts have been given to each of us, "But the manifestation of the Spirit is given to each one for the profit *of all:* for to one is given the word of wisdom through the Spirit, to another the word of knowledge through the same Spirit, to another faith by the same Spirit, to another gifts of healing by the same Spirit, to another the working of miracles, to another prophecy, to another discerning of spirits, to another *different* kinds of tongues, to another the interpretation of tongues."

One of the greatest benefits of fulfilling our God-given calling is that the question of what constitutes true success is finally answered. A paradigm shift (paradigm: a philosophical and theoretical framework of a scientific school or discipline within which theories, laws, and generalizations and the experiments performed in support of them are formulated; a philosophical or theoretical framework of any kind. Shift: to exchange for or replace by another: to change the place, position, or direction of) has to take place in the collective hearts and minds of those in leadership and those of us who are earnestly following Christ.

Relating to God as a harsh taskmaster opens the door for thousands of other misperceptions. There are still millions of *believers* who are mistakenly convinced that God does not want them to be successful. The flip side of that is just as poorly conceived. The idea that our works will score brownie points with God and that we in some way need to beat out the competition drives home the point that we have been sold a bill of goods and we have bought into it hook, line, and sinker. The premise that success is measured by how well we do compared to how others do is not only frustrating, it is completely the antithesis of Who God is and who we are in Him. That mindset completely negates His character and our Christ-likeness.

Regardless of how well we do in any spiritual or natural exercise, someone else will always do it better or worse. However, when we define success in terms of God's purpose, for our lives, the standard changes completely. True success is not what we have done compared to someone else, but rather what we have done compared to what God has assigned us to accomplish within our limited time frame on the earth. As individuals, we are all given unique talents to accomplish the assignments He has asked us to fulfill. We all have specific things to do with the same opportunities to experience His blessings as we endeavor to accomplish them.

It Is About Completing, Not Competing

In John 19:30 Jesus is the best example of how we are to live this out. He understood that He had succeeded because He finished the work His Father had sent Him to do. He had completed His course. Walking in our calling means we do not have to compare our spiritual or natural gifts to others. Completing, not competing, is what demonstrates to a lost and dying world that we are true followers of Christ and that we get it that our gifts are for mankind, not for selfish ambitions. The coolest part about living life according to this plan is that as we use those gifts to bless others, we become not only wildly successful (in God's eyes) but we have the side benefit of living a deeply satisfying existence.

Sadly, it is in this very area that many believers begin to compare their walk, gift, calling, and instruction to another's. We want somebody to teach us and lead us in obedience, but God does not have grandchildren—He only has children. We have to learn to hear and respond to God's voice based on *our* intimate relationship to Him. Just as in Exodus 20:19 when the Israelites asked Moses to hear from God for them, we would rather get our instructions and directions from someone other than God. The Israelites found that it was much easier to believe that Moses had missed it if things went wrong than take responsibility for themselves. All of these years later Christians still have that same mentality. If we hear from man instead of God, the responsibility for failure can always be traced back to whoever we heard it from. However, when God speaks directly to us, we have two choices, obey or disobey.

Many may not believe it but God really does speak to each of us as individuals. For those who do believe that God speaks to them, you know how we are when God actually does speak to us directly about an issue, situation, or circumstance. Like you, when I do blow it (as I often do), I immediately ask, "God, is that You?" I know full well Who it is. I know it is God, but I still ask and then try to find a way out. "If it is really You, God, then give me a Scripture." God will give me a Scripture such as Hebrews 10:39 that encourages me to remember who I am in Christ, "You are not of those who go back to destruction." The point is that God is concerned only about my well-being. God is not concerned about whatever wrong choice it may have been, He is concerned about *me*.

So often we listen to whatever message or revelation is being taught and never research the teaching for ourselves. 2 Timothy 2: 13-15 instructs us to study the Word of God to go deeper into scripture and confirm that it is sound doctrine and biblically based. Sadly, the Bible is like that book in the dashboard of our cars. We listen to our mechanic but never read the owner's manual for ourselves so that we know how to maintain our vehicles to maximum performance.

My personal experience with my loving and giving heavenly Father did not correspond with many of the teachings that I had heard, so I started reading the Bible for myself. I learned that there is always a reason for God's chastening regardless of the circumstances I find myself in. The bottom line is that He wants His people to live blessed lives. Hebrews 12:8 tells us, "If you weren't My son, I would not be chastening you, only bastards do not get chastened. You are My son. If you weren't Mine, I would not be chastening you, but you are and I want you to be blessed, so please obey Me."

God deals with all of us differently. There may be things God has been speaking to you about dealing with once and for all. The good news about this great God that we serve is that whatever He has been talking to you about is for your benefit not because He wants to punish you. 1 Chronicles 16:25 reminds us that He is a great God and worthy to be praised and that He is to be revered above all other gods.

The key to being obedient to God is having a relationship with Him. We obey because we love Him and He loves us. John 14:15-17 states, "If you love Me, keep My commandments." It does not say love Me because you are afraid of Me.

Obedience Brings Rewards

Every obedient act brings a reward. Hebrews 11:6 tells us, "He that comes to God must believe that He is God, and that He rewards those who diligently seek Him." Isn't it good that God gives rewards? John 14:21 makes still another promise, "He who has My commandments, and keeps them, it is he who loves Me, and he who loves Me will be loved by My Father, and I will love him and manifest Myself to him." Manifest means to: exhibit, disclose, appear, declare, and inform.

God will declare Himself to us when we obey Him. 2 Chronicles 16:9 tells us that God is looking to and fro across the whole earth for somebody who is obeying Him so He can show Himself strong on their behalf. He is looking for those who are obedient so He can show His power and disclose His mysteries to them. God will manifest Himself as we obey Him. Acts 5:32 tells us, "The Holy Spirit is given to those who obey. We are His witnesses to these things, and the Holy Spirit, whom God has given to those who obey Him."

If we desire to walk more closely with the Holy Spirit, with more of God's power and anointing in our lives, then we have to start obeying God in small things. As we walk in obedience, He will entrust us with more responsibility, authority, and accountability. Many of us do not realize that God is speaking all the time. The question we should be asking is, "Are we listening?" Most of the time we dismiss His voice as something else, but God really does direct our paths.

Obedience is for our good. We have to learn to listen to that still, small voice that is on the inside of us. That is the obedience God wants us to walk in. Every time we obey it will result in blessings and lead to good success in life.

Amazing Grace

Once while I was preaching at a barn revival in Skiatook, Oklahoma, there were about four hundred and sixty real cowboys wearing cowboy hats and spurs. The majority of the attendees that evening were un-churched people. As the worship service began, we started to sing *Amazing Grace,* and a couple walked to the altar and began slow dancing. I am not talking about waltzing . . . but *"slow"* dancing. I was not sure how to handle it but the Lord said, "Leave them alone." They danced the whole song. After the song, they sat down, and I preached.

When it came time for the altar call, they came to the altar and sobbingly gave this testimony: "We have never been in church and we were about to get a divorce, but when we heard that song, *Amazing Grace*, something moved in our hearts, and the only thing we knew to do was what we always did when we were in love. So, that is why we started dancing to the song." God met them right where they were, filled them with the Holy Spirit, and saved their marriage, all in a barn that night. If I had interrupted, I could have blown what God was doing in their lives. He spoke, I obeyed, and their lives were radically changed.

Obedience always brings a reward. Isaiah 1:18-19 states, "If you be willing, and obedient, you will eat the good of the land." Job 36:11 assures us, "If you will obey Me and serve Me, you will spend your days in prosperity, and your years in pleasure." I Peter 1:22 goes even further, "You purify your souls through obedience." As we obey, it brings purification to our souls. As we begin to walk in obedience, God openly rewards us. Deuteronomy 28:1 tells us, "Now, it shall come to pass, that if you diligently obey the voice of the Lord your God to observe carefully all His commands, which I command you today, the Lord your God will set you high above all nations of the earth, and all these blessing shall come on you, and overtake you, because you obeyed the voice of the Lord your God. Blessed shall you be in the city. Blessed shall you be in the country. Blessed shall be the fruit of your body, and the produce of your ground, and the increase of your herds, and the increase of your cattle, and the offspring of your flock."

In contemporary terms that tells us that we will have Kelloggs in the cupboard, meat in the freezer, and our children will be blessed. Verse five elaborates, "Blessed shall be your basket and kneading bowl. Blessed shall you be when you come in, and blessed shall you be when you go out. The Lord will cause your enemies aroused against you to be defeated before your face. They shall come against you one way, and flee seven ways."

Those are the promises of God and are our reward when we are obedient to the voice of God. "The Lord will command His blessing upon you in the storehouse and all that you set your hand to. He will bless you in the land which the Lord God is giving you. The Lord will establish you as a holy people to Himself, just as He has sworn to you, if you will keep His commandments. All the peoples of the earth will say that you are called by the Lord, and the Lord will grant you plenty of goods, fruit of body, increase of livestock, produce and ground, which the Lord God gave you. The Lord will open His good treasures in heaven to give you rain in season, and bless all the many works of your hands. You will lend to many nations, not borrow, and the Lord will make you the head, not the tail, above, not beneath, if you will heed the commandments of the Lord your God." From God's perspective, obedience is better than sacrifice.

I have learned that I can get more done by obeying God than by sacrificing something that will produce only temporal rewards. When we find the will of God and are obedient, good things will happen for us and we will enjoy good success God's way. Our mentality is that a sacrifice brings the blessing of God. I take my cue from King Saul's impatience in 1 Samuel 15-22, "And Samuel said, 'Has the Lord as great delight in burnt offerings and sacrifices, as in obeying the voice of the Lord? Behold, to obey is better than sacrifice, and to hearken than the fat of rams.'"

When we give in obedience to what God is asking of us we will be rewarded by living in the blessings He has promised us. Jesus was the Sacrifice when He died on the Cross. The Old Covenant was replaced by the New Covenant, and it is our obedience that God honors.

One Day of Favor Is Better

One day of favor really is better than a thousand years of labor. When we obey, we start living in the favor of God and He will do things for us that we cannot do for ourselves. My wife understood that revelation long before I did. She will do some wild things in obedience to what she believes God has spoken to her.

Once I came home from a mission trip and all of the furniture in the living room was gone. We did not have the nicest stuff in the world, but it was in very good shape and at the very least was something to sit on. We were trusting God to replace it, but frankly better furniture meant more to her than it did me. After my initial shock she explained to me how we happened to be furniture-less. She had met a missionary couple who did not have anything and her heart melted for them. She believed God spoke to her to give them our living room furniture. I asked, "And you gave it to them? Didn't He say keep a couch?" I mean, it was bare carpet. She said, "I had to obey God, I knew it was Him." I said, "OK, praise God."

A couple of days later I walked into my office and there was a furniture magazine on my desk with a check in it. God had spoken to a lady, who did not know what Bev had done, but she was obedient to what she believed God had spoken to her and she gave us a check and told us to go buy new furniture and be blessed. She had heard from God to buy us new furniture. The really wild thing about it was how specific God was. The magazine was turned to a beautiful set of white leather furniture which is exactly what my wife wanted and exactly what we bought with that check. Not only did we get blessed by giving, we were blessed with better furniture than we had before, and more of it.

God wanted to do something for us and He wants to do something for you. If we will start being a blessing, we will be blessed. God's blessings will start flowing in our lives and we will accomplish things we could never accomplish on our own.

When God first spoke to me about moving to Alabama, we had no idea that we would hear from Him to start the church that is now Word Alive International Outreach. I was in the midst of one of the darkest times in my life. It was definitely the darkest since salvation. For weeks I had battled health issues which led to financial problems that ultimately had my mind in such torment that I did not know if I was coming or going.

I continued to travel around the world preaching, but it seemed as though God was a million miles away. After I returned from a trip to Europe, God woke me in the very early hours of the morning and spoke to me about moving from Florida to Alabama. I told Bev, "Wake up, honey, we are moving to Alabama!" She asked, "What do you mean?" I repeated what I believed God had just told me about moving. Her reaction was not what I had hoped to hear; however, because of the prevailing circumstances it was appropriate. She said, "You do not know who is talking to you right now, go back to sleep."

Well, God had spoken and we did move to Alabama. Then God said, "Build a church in Coldwater. Build it and they will come." Who would have thought that God was going to birth a church in Coldwater, Alabama that in just a few short years would have 4,500 plus regular attendees, with thousands saved, healed, delivered, and water baptized? We obeyed God, took a step of faith, and we have seen the fruit of our obedience.

A Lifestyle of Obedience

Luke 6:46-49 describes the protection of living a lifestyle of obedience: "But why do you call Me 'Lord, Lord,' and not do the things which I say? Whoever comes to Me, and hears My sayings and does them, I will show you whom he is like: He is like a man building a house, who dug deep and laid the foundation on the rock. And when the flood arose, the stream beat vehemently against that house, and could not shake it, for it was founded on the rock. But he who heard and did nothing is like a man who built a house on the earth without a foundation, against which the stream beat vehemently; and immediately it fell. And the ruin of that house was great."

When we are obedient we will be placed on such a strong foundation that no matter what storm comes our way our house will not be shaken. The key to this portion of Scripture is this: *One who hears and obeys.* Two heard, but only one obeyed. God will never hold us accountable for what we did not understand or we did not hear. He will make sure that we hear correctly and will give us the opportunity to obey or disobey. He who obeys is like a strong foundation. When the storms of life blow and things get out of whack, our house is going to stand because we have chosen to obey God.

When we obey Him our lives become filled with power and we become full of God's strength. Things will not shake us up or move us.

When we keep His commands we will have long life, length of days, and peace. I looked at that recently and thought, how powerful is that, when we are obedient we will have long life and length of days? I thought they were the same, but it cannot be. Why would He say it twice? Long life means the number of years. Length of days means you will get more done than you would have otherwise because your days have been lengthened. I believe when we obey God we really do have the capacity to accomplish more than most people. That makes perfect sense if, in fact, we *are* getting more done by being obedient to God's will. The other benefits to obedience are length of days and peace. We will live longer *and* be at peace with God and man when we live a lifestyle of obedience to God's Word.

What a great feeling it is to lay my head down at night, in peace, even though I may not have gotten everything right during the course of the day, but to know I obeyed God, to the best of my ability. What does that mean? That means when I make a mistake, I apologize. When I do something wrong, I repent for it. At the end of the day I am in the will of God, I have obeyed Him, and when I lie down, my sleep is sweet. When I get up in the morning I know there are new mercies waiting for me and new opportunities to hear from God and to live in obedience to His will for my life.

Every step of obedience I take brings another blessing to my life. The greatest way to enjoy good success is to determine we are going to live a life of obedience. For some of us that may mean we lay this book down and go call someone and say, "Please forgive me or I forgive you." God may be asking you to do some things that will catapult you into His promises and cycle of blessings.

Many times we disobey God because of the fear of man. That is what happened to King Saul in I Samuel 13:6-14, "When the men of Israel saw that they were in danger (for the people were distressed), then the people hid in caves, in thickets, in rocks, in holes, and in pits. And some of the Hebrews crossed over the Jordan to the land of Gad and Gilead.

As for Saul, he was still in Gilgal, and all the people followed him trembling. Then he waited seven days, according to the time set by Samuel. But Samuel did not come to Gilgal; and the people were scattered from him. So Saul said, "Bring a burnt offering and peace offerings here to me." And he offered the burnt offering. Now it happened, as soon as he had finished presenting the burnt offering, that Samuel came; and Saul went out to meet him, that he might greet him. And Samuel said, "What have you done?" Saul said, "When I saw that the people were scattered from me, and that you did not come within the days appointed, and that the Philistines gathered together at Michmash, then I said, 'The Philistines will now come down on me at Gilgal, and I have not made supplication to the Lord.' Therefore I felt compelled, and offered a burnt offering." And Samuel said to Saul, "You have done foolishly. You have not kept the commandment of the Lord your God, which He commanded you. For now the Lord would have established your kingdom over Israel forever. But now your kingdom shall not continue. The Lord has sought for Himself a man after His own heart, and the Lord has commanded him to be commander over His people, because you have not kept what the Lord commanded you."

Saul did not obey God because he was afraid of what people would say. Do not let fear keep you from obeying God. It may be terrifying at first, but there is a blessing on the other side of whatever God is asking us to do. The possibilities are limitless. There may be a relationship in your life that God wants to intervene in and restore. He may be asking you to give of your resources. It may be time for you to answer the call to ministry and missions. It may be as simple as praying for or encouraging someone that you know who needs it.

Many of us know what a blessing it is for God to ask something of us and see the fruit of obeying Him right away. However, many of us have yet to experience God in that perspective. God changes us as we are obedient to give somebody a hug and tell them we have been thinking of and praying for them. It impacts the person we have demonstrated God's love and character to, and it encourages us to move quickly when God speaks.

It is so encouraging when we take a step of faith and obey God. It may seem like a small thing, but God will begin to give you long life and length of days as you obey His Word. I have come to realize that delayed obedience is disobedience. God wants us to respond when He asks us to do something.

I believe there is coming a day in the nation in which we live that obedience may be a life or death choice. That is why we need to train ourselves to hear God now. There may come a time, in the United States, when we wake up and not know what is waiting for us when we step out of our homes. We will have to hear the Voice of God for clear direction. It is now, in the days of peace, that we need to train ourselves to hear and obey God. I pray that God will give us a spirit of obedience so we hear His voice clearly when He speaks and that we obey quickly because only good will happen as we walk in obedience to the Voice of God.

Favor Really Ain't Fair

Favor: A special privilege or right granted or conceded.

Chapter Three

While researching the Word to write this book, I came to the conclusion that if we did not have another chapter in the Bible other than Proverbs Chapter Three, we could live with clear direction for our lives and in God's will in all of our relationships. The whole chapter is so clear, but Proverbs 3:3 is especially specific about how to walk in godly relationships. "Let not mercy and truth forsake you. Bind them around your neck. Write them upon the table of your heart, and so find favor and high esteem in the sight of God and man." That verse tells us there is a way we can find favor and high esteem in the sight of God and man.

When we actively pursue the things of God not only will we have favor and high esteem with God, but He will cause us to have favor and high esteem with men. Why is it important to have favor, not only with God, but with men? It is important because the earth is the Lord's and the fullness thereof but He has given it unto the hands of men. We not only need to have favor with God, we also need to have favor with men. Allowing mercy and truth to flow through our lives begins to release favor.

Without the truth, we will never receive mercy. Without mercy, we will never be able to handle the truth. Many of us have experienced ministry that brings truth yet is void of mercy. When we hear only the truth without mercy it becomes legalism. I read this observation by acclaimed author Max Lucado recently and it seems to drive home why we want to avoid legalism in any form. "Legalism is a slow suffocation of the Spirit and the amputation of one's dreams." When we hear only about mercy without truth, it becomes lawlessness. God does not want us to live in legalism and He does not want us to live in lawlessness. God wants us to have a revelation of mercy and truth so we can walk in the favor of God.

In John 1:17 this truth is expounded upon, "The law came by Moses but grace and truth through Jesus Christ." Psalm 85:10 confirms that, "Mercy and truth have met together. Righteousness and peace have kissed." Jesus is mercy and truth. Moses was given the law so that Jesus could fulfill it. Moses told the Israelites what to do, but the law left little room for failure. Truth without mercy will tell you the truth of the condition you are in but gives you no power to change. When we demonstrate mercy with truth it not only reveals the truth of who we are, but it also gives us a way out. When Jesus came in mercy and truth, He placed us right between the lips of God where righteousness and peace kissed each other. When we understand how righteousness and peace was poured into our lives by Jesus' death on the Cross, it changes everything.

Satan will lie to us and tell us not to expose the truth of our wrong choices. When we hide a sin it causes us to live in fear, guilt, condemnation, and judgment. Sadly, our churches have been so judgmental, full of condemnation and sometimes even contempt for those who are not at the same place of spiritual awareness that we are, that we forget we once needed, and still do, the same measure of mercy they now need.

The enemy of our souls likes nothing more than when believers judge each other and prevent deliverance from taking place because of the fear of man. If condemnation keeps one person from allowing the truth about their sin, situation, circumstance, or issue from reaching the surface where it can be exposed to God's mercy and truth, then the enemy's lies have prevailed. The more we confess our sins, the greater mercy we will receive from God.

If we would lay down our foolish pride and stop worrying about what everybody thinks of us, we would be more than halfway through most of our problems. I figured out a long time ago that it does not really matter what anybody thinks. I want more of the mercy of God and I will do whatever it takes to receive it. If it means being open, honest, and transparent, then that is what I am going to be. The more I confess my weaknesses and shortcomings, the more mercy God extends to me. The more I realize what I cannot do, the more God shows me what I can. When we walk in truth and receive His mercy and love, God's favor will rest on us.

Proverbs 28:13 reads, "He who covers his sin will not prosper." One of the most important principles of experiencing good success is confessing our sins. It is human nature to want to hide our weaknesses, but we will never enjoy the good success of God when we do because it is God's desire that we have His nature. As we mature into transparent believers, willing to openly express and confess our sins, shortcomings, and secrets, we will become a person who is willing to turn to God and receive His great mercy. He who covers his sins will not prosper, but whoever confesses and forsakes them, will have mercy.

How many ministries and lives could have been saved and spared if those in peril had felt the liberty to be open and honest? It is like the three preachers who got together and said, 'Let's be open and honest with one another.' One of them said, "OK, I have a problem with lust and I want to confess that to you gentlemen today." The other preacher confessed, "Well, I have a problem with money. I'm not much of a manager, and I've taken some money inappropriately in the church." A big sorrowful expression came on the face of the third preacher who said, "I have a big problem with gossiping." They had told the wrong guy, hadn't they? The moral of the story is be led by the Holy Spirit to be open with someone who has a solution who is not superficial.

Love Your Neighbor as Yourself

Regretfully, the church and the world do not look too different when it comes to gossiping and judging one another. Loving one another as ourselves certainly is not as prevalent as one would think. We do not extend mercy yet we perceive that we deserve to receive it. It would seem that as the Body of Christ we have never really embraced the revelation of God's truth and commandments to love God with all of our hearts and our neighbors as ourselves. How much more will our heavenly Father, Who loves us, be merciful to us if we confess our sins and begin to love God with all of our hearts and our neighbors as ourselves?

As we begin to walk in truth and demonstrate mercy, we will begin to live in freedom. When that happens we also begin to walk in the favor of God. Proverbs 3:3-4 is clear, "Do not let mercy and truth forsake you. Do not let them run away from you. Hold on to them. Tie them around your neck. Write them on the tablet of your heart. Keep them close to you at all times, because if you will, you will find great favor with Me." The reward of God's blessing is in direct proportion to our obedience to walk in mercy and truth. As we begin to exercise this Kingdom principle, we will really begin to enjoy the favor of God.

It is difficult to grasp (and hard for many to believe) that the favor of God is in direct proportion to the mercy and truth we give others. Salvation is free. We cannot do anything to get saved. It is freely given and was bought by the price that Jesus paid on the Cross to redeem us from our sins. However, we can increase the favor of God on our lives by sowing mercy and truth into others.

God does have preferred customers, frequent flyers if you will. On airlines around the world when you are a frequent flyer, you get preferential treatment. That is really what favor means . . . preferential treatment. So, God does have favorites. That is really true. I am not making it up. You may say you thought God was no respecter of persons. That is also true, but there are people who have more favor than others. It is because they have a revelation of God's grace and they have extended mercy and truth more than judgment and condemnation. I realize it seems as though I have placed a challenge on the table, but through Scripture I will demonstrate that we can increase the favor of God on our lives. Luke 2:52 clearly states, "Jesus increased in wisdom, in stature, and in favor with God and man." The *Bible* tells us that Jesus grew and increased in favor with God and with man.

Luke 6:35-38 has been taught as if it was about money, but it is not—it is about mercy. "Love your enemies. Do good and lend, hoping for nothing in return, and your reward will be great. You will be sons of the Most High, for He is kind to the unthankful and the evil. Therefore, be merciful, just as your Father in heaven is merciful. Judge not and ye shall not be judged. Condemn not, and you will not be condemned. Forgive and you will be forgiven. Give and it shall be given to you, good measure, pressed down, shaken together, running over will be put into your bosom. For with the same measure you use it, it's going to be measured back to you again." The Word states that if we judge, we are going to be judged. If we condemn, we are going to be condemned, but if we will be merciful, it will be given back to us, good measure, pressed down, shaken together and running over. Moreover, it is God that will give the same mercy we have shown back to us

I want the kind of favor that is found in Luke 6:38, "Good measure, pressed down, shaken together and running over on my life." The Word is very specific that the same measure we use will be measured back. If we judge, it is going to come back to us as judgment, good measure, pressed down, shaken together, and running over. If we demonstrate mercy and grace, it will be given back to us good measure, pressed down, shaken together and running over. We really do have the capability to increase the favor or the judgment of God in our lives. We can literally determine it by the measure of mercy and grace we have for others.

Of course, we want everybody to speak the truth to us in love, and we want to speak the truth to everybody else with just truth. That is why it is so easy for mercy and truth to be received but not extended. God promises that if we live according to His Word concerning these things, then we will have favor. What exactly is favor? Favor is special, preferential treatment from God. Favor opens doors, releases finances, and favor causes us to be at the right place at the right time. Even the small things that occur will be blessed when we are living in the favor of God.

Not too long ago I was in a department store and found a pair of name brand pants that were exactly my size, for one dollar. I was at the right place at the right time. It may not seem as though God is interested in little things, but God is not so big that He cannot do little things and He is not too little that He will not do big things in our lives when we trust Him. I want the favor of God in every area of my life, small and large.

Many of us have not yet had a breakthrough in this area. Yet the principle of sowing and reaping is just as applicable to demonstrating mercy and grace as it is to tithing and giving offerings. If we keep sowing mercy and truth, as opposed to judgment and condemnation, the favor of God will begin to overtake us. It will happen in unexpected ways such as getting a promotion when in the natural someone else is in line for it, or maybe the deal that seemed as if it would never go through happens at the exact right time. These are examples of big things, but God really is interested even in small things.

It's the Small Things

A few years ago I was traveling in Zimbabwe, Africa. I walked into a hotel and met a preacher who had on the most beautiful pair of shoes. I said, "Those are really nice shoes." He said, "Thank you very much." Six months later, I was in Detroit, Michigan sitting on the platform at a crusade and a guy walked up to me and said, "I need to see you after the service." I said, "OK." I had never met him before in my life. He said, "Be out in front of your hotel at two o'clock." I was standing out in front of the hotel at two o'clock, thinking that he wanted to get a message to my employer. He picked me up and as we began driving down the road he said, "I own a shoe manufacturing company. The Lord spoke to me and said to give you a pair of shoes."

It did not take me long to realize that this was the same place where the man in Africa had gotten his shoes. God's attention to details never ceases to amaze me; from Zimbabwe to Detroit is a long way. Why would God be interested enough in a small thing like shoes and speak to a businessman over a thousand miles away to hear His Voice about a desire in my heart, orchestrate the whole deal, and bless me like that? There is only one answer: It is His favor.

When we arrived at the manufacturing plant, I realized that there were literally thousands of pairs of shoes available to me, but alas, not the pair I saw in Zimbabwe. I thought, "Well this cannot be God after all. Surely He would not orchestrate all this and then say He could not get that particular pair for me. Finally after looking and looking I described the pair I had seen. He said that not only did they not have any more of that particular style, but they did not even manufacture that shoe any longer. That had just registered when all of a sudden the doors opened from the back and a guy came through with a box of shoes and said, "I found a pair. They are size 10 ½." I said, "Giddy up, they are my size!"

Now, shoes are shoes, but if God will arrange for me to get a specific pair of shoes, how much more will He do to save, deliver, heal, get us out of debt, restore marriages, bless our children and our businesses, or give us favor to get the things that we need?

We do not serve a God that has ears that cannot hear or eyes that cannot see. He saw a little desire in my heart and orchestrated all sorts of circumstances to get a pair of shoes for me. That is called favor. God will take us places we have never been, get us things we could not get on our own, and demonstrate Himself to be strong on our behalf. We can start enjoying the blessings and favor of God when we start sowing mercy and truth.

Once on a trip in Ukraine, my friend Sai Mudiam was traveling with me, and we realized his passport was not in order. As we entered Ukraine through customs, Sai was detained. He does not speak any Ukrainian and they did not speak any English. The rest of the team had already passed through customs and he was still being held. The officials would not let me go back and they would not let him go forward. Nobody spoke English, so I just started hollering, "Call the President! Call the President! Somebody call the President!" Another one of the team told me to shut up before they shot us with their machine guns.

We had to fight tooth and nail, get an interpreter, and offer money just to get him in. We finally got him across the border and proceeded with the mission trip. Before we left for the flight home, we asked God to give us favor as we did not want to leave him in Ukraine. We arrived for the flight and we were checking our bags through. We were in a long line, and out of nowhere a lady walked up to me and asked, "Are you VIPs?" I answered, "Yes." She said, "Come with me." I thought, "I do not know where we are going or who we are supposed to be, but we are going to enjoy it."

She took us into a private lounge with coffee and food, checked and tagged our bags for us, and told us to make ourselves comfortable. We were wondering who we were supposed to be so we could pretend to be them. We sat there, enjoyed the favor of God, and thanked Him for blessing us. We later found out that they had allowed us to go through special customs for VIPs *because of* Sai's passport. Instead of harassing us, they passed us right through. We knew then that not only had God blessed us, He had demonstrated His favor.

Favor Ain't Fair

Favor is receiving things we do not ask for. It is something we reap because we have already sown mercy and truth. When we are kind to one another, we are living a life of extending mercy and truth. As we do for others what they cannot do for themselves, God will do things for us that we cannot do for ourselves. That is why the Bible reminds us in Proverbs 3:27 that if we have it in the power of our hand to do good, then do it. If we do something for someone that they cannot do for themselves, God will do something for us we cannot do for ourselves.

Psalm 89:18 states, "Favor will bring you strength. My horn shall be exalted with favor." Psalm 30: 5, 11 continues, "Favor will turn weeping into joy. His anger is but for a moment, but in His favor is life. He has turned my mourning into dancing. Weeping endures for the night, but joy comes in the morning." Psalm 30:7 makes it even clearer, "God makes favor and causes your mountain to stand strong." Psalm 5:12 states, "Favor will bring divine protection. The righteous shall be surrounded by a shield of favor and blessings." Daniel 9:23 lets us know we are not alone. Because of favor angels will be released to protect us.

In Daniel 10: 13 an angel arrived on the scene and said, "Hey, highly favored one. I have come because of your prayers." He introduced himself as Michael, then explained he had actually heard Daniel's prayer twenty-one days prior to his arrival but had to fight demonic powers to get through to him. The good news is that because of the favor of God, angels will start fighting on your behalf.

Do you remember the story of Mary, Jesus' mother in Luke 1:28-30? Scripture retells how the angel of God came to her and said, "You are highly favored. You have FOUND favor." That tells us that she was *looking* for God's blessings and favor. She did something that got God's attention and attracted the favor of God to her. In Genesis 6: 8 Noah FOUND favor. In Exodus 33: 12-13. Moses FOUND favor. They were all actively looking for God's favor. Even if we do not understand the principle of sowing truth and mercy, when they are extended, we are actively seeking favor, and we will receive it. When we sow mercy and truth, we will walk in favor and blessing. When we live in obedience to His Word, demonstrate God's character and seek His favor, we will find it.

The Book of Esther is the story of a orphaned girl who was called by God to become a queen. Like many of us she was called to a very specific time and season to affect and influence the Kingdom of God. It was her destiny to deliver her people from destruction. Many believers in the Kingdom today are called, just as Esther was, for such a time as this. Christians around the world are beginning to fulfill their destinies to prevent God's people from being destroyed. God does have an economy in the Kingdom and when we get involved with God and His economics, living and operating in them, favor will start propelling us to our destiny.

As the story of Esther's rise to influence unfolds, we see her stepping into an arena of power, politics, and position that she could not possibly have foreseen as a part of her life. Moreover, in the natural, she could not possibly have been prepared for the circumstances that she had to contend with. Yet not only did she contend with persecution, problems, and pessimism, she conquered them.

As we open our hearts to the purpose and plan God has for us, just like Esther, we may sometimes find ourselves in places that only God could have taken us to. If we see these circumstances as part of God's plan for our lives, we will recognize it is the favor of God positioning us to be blessed. Just like Queen Esther, the favor of God will be the only reason we are there. Esther 5:2 tells of the king's scepter being stretched toward Esther, allowing her entrance to his throne. The favor of God allows us access to Him.

Preferred Flyers

In airports there are two lines, a long line for those who do not fly very often and a short line for those who do. All the preferred flyers are in the short line. When I pray, I want to be in the short line. When I call on God, I want Him to put somebody on hold and answer my call. Favor places us in the short line. I believe in favor in little things. I always have favor in parking lots. Because I am usually in a hurry, I like to park close to the entrance of the store I am going to. I may have to circle a couple of times, but I eventually park in front. Believe it or not, God really is interested in that sort of stuff. The key is to be willing to give up the good parking space on occasion and bless someone else with it. God will give you another one and you have created an opportunity to be on the giving end which places us in the position to receive God's favor.

God has so many creative ways to demonstrate His favor. One night after service my wife and I went to eat with friends. There is a little restaurant on one side and a bar on the other side in the place we chose. We were eating on the restaurant side and the guy who was playing in the bar stopped playing and walked over to us. He said, "We are closing. May I play a song so you can dance?" I answered, "Sure, what would you like to play?" He said, "Unforgettable." That is a great song and also happens to be one of my wife's favorites. As the beautiful music started to fill the room my wife and I began to dance.

In just a few moments the server was in tears. She said, "I was so sad until I saw you dancing with your wife, and then I felt joy. Please pray for me because I want the peace of God back in my life. My husband and I are going through a very hard time." We wrapped our arms around her and began to pray for the peace of God to be hers once again. Right there in the restaurant she made the one decision that could really change her life and that was to follow Jesus.

A great biblical example of favor is the life of King David. He had a heart after God, so I have really studied his life. Isaiah 55:3-10 tells us something interesting about David's example for the people, "Listen carefully to Me, and eat *what is* good, and let your soul delight itself in abundance. Incline your ear, and come to Me. Hear, and your soul shall live; and I will make an everlasting covenant with you, *the sure mercies of David*. Indeed I have given him *as* a witness to the people, a leader and commander for the people. Surely you shall call a nation you do not know, and nations who do not know you shall run to you, because of the Lord your God, and the Holy One of Israel; for He has glorified you." Seek the Lord while He may be found, call upon Him while He is near. Let the wicked forsake his way, and the unrighteous man his thoughts; let him return to the Lord, and He will have mercy on him; and to our God, for He will abundantly pardon. "For My thoughts are not your thoughts, nor are your ways My ways," says the Lord. "For as the heavens are higher than the earth, so are My ways higher than your ways, and My thoughts than your thoughts."

God began to speak to me about the sure mercies of David and what that really means. How did David attract such favor on his life? In I Samuel 16:12 David was chosen over his brothers but how did that happen? In the natural he certainly did not seem to be the likely candidate. The answer is simple, God touches many people, but if you ever touch Him your life will be marked with favor.

Attract the Favor of God

When no one was looking and he was alone in the pasture, David worshipped God and sang love songs to Him. God must have said, "I like that guy." David began to attract the favor of God through his pure adoration and worshipful heart. God touches many people and they are blessed, but touch Him just once, when no one is looking, and you will be marked forever by God's favor. God marked David with favor and He never let mercy and truth forsake him. David understood that he was in the position that he was in only by the mercy of God. With that understanding he kept on serving his brothers. Next, we read of David who at first was found to be very pleasing to King Saul, but before too much time had passed jealousy had stolen their relationship and Saul desired to kill David and began to pursue him to kill him

While the chase was on David had several opportunities to kill Saul. He was so close one time he cut a section from his robe. That is how close he was to the king, but he never laid a hand on him. He was merciful. After Saul died, David implored the captains of the army saying, "Please do not publish it in Gath and tell it not to the Philistines." After years of being wrongfully judged and persecuted, David did not want Saul defamed.

In the years to come, even after David had made wrong choices and been on the receiving end of God's mercies, he never forgot the House of Saul. Saul's only remaining heir, Mephibosheth, who had been crippled as a small boy, was brought to him and ate at the king's table all the days of his life. David, who was now king, adopted him and was merciful to Saul's son.

After years of experiencing God's favor, David wanted to build God a house, but God said, "No, I am going to build you a house." When God's favor is with us, we learn that we cannot out bless Him. Sometimes in restaurants we see grown men or women fighting over who is going to pay the check. They both want to bless each other. That is what happens when we start walking with God. You want to bless Him, but He wants to do something for you. Then David said, "Who am I? Who is my father's house that you should show me such preferential treatment?" God responded and said, "I know My servant."

Mistaken Identity

Do you know what favor really is? It is mistaken identity and it really ain't fair. When we live in God's blessings and favor it is because we have touched God by showing mercy and grace to someone that God wanted to bless. It is not because of who we are, where we came from, or what our pedigree is. It is simply because of the grace, favor, and mercy of God. Psalm 18:26 tells us something very powerful, "With the merciful, I will show Myself merciful. With the blameless I will show Myself blameless. With the pure I will show Myself pure. But, with the devious I will show Myself shrewd."

I do not want God to have to think shrewdly *about* me. I desire for God to be shrewd *for* me. James 4: 6 tells us, "God resists the proud, but gives grace to the humble." That is a powerful statement. He fights the proud. It does not mean He will not bless us, but it does mean He will fight us if we are proud. He gives mercy, grace, and favor to the humble, and when we write grace and mercy in our hearts, God's favor will be with us.

At the end of the day I want to be held in high esteem with God. It does not really matter what men think. It is not always convenient to be merciful and it is not always convenient to tell the truth, but if we will the Bible is very specific that we will be held in high esteem with God and have great favor not only with Him, but with men. God will begin to do things for us that we cannot do for ourselves. He will reverse situations in our lives that seem impossible simply because of His favor, grace and mercy.

Who's Your Daddy?

Daddy: Father

Chapter Four

I hope that you are beginning to understand how exciting it is that God's will is for us to prosper and to be blessed in every area of our lives—, emotionally, financially and physically. It is rewarding to learn that God's promise in Joshua 1:8 is for us as well, "This Book of the Law shall not depart from your mouth, but you shall meditate in it day and night, that you may observe to do according to all that is written in it. For then you will make your way prosperous, and then you will have good success." That promise is just as relevant now as it was then. Proverbs 3:5-6 states, "Trust in the Lord with all your heart, lean not to your own understanding. In all your ways acknowledge Him and He shall direct your paths." As believers that should be the revelation that we have built our foundation of trust in God on. As we acknowledge Him, He will direct our paths.

Learning to trust God is one of, if not the most, important keys to good success. Our natural tendency is to be in control of everything. It is part of our nature to desire to be in control of our future, finances, and family. The list could continue to infinity. Sometimes we just have to be out of control and let God have it. We have to relinquish the reins and let God be God.

We have a tendency to hang on tightly to everything. Proverbs 3:4-6 tells us, "Lean on, trust in, be confident in the Lord with all your heart and mind, and do not rely on your own insight or understanding. In all your ways, recognize and acknowledge Him, and He will direct and make straight and plain your paths. Trust God that He will look after you, do for you, and guide you according to His power and not your own."

We tend to trust God for a while, but when the pressure is on, things are not happening on the time schedule that we have subconsciously put God on, and things aren't coming together, our reasoning skills kick in and before we know it we have put God in the wind and made decisions that we will come to regret. Then, not only do we still have the same old issue, but we now have a whole new set of problems that were caused by our impatience. We are then left trying to figure out how in the world we got in this mess in the first place.

I always try to figure out God. How is He going to do it, when is He going to do it, is He going to do anything at all, and what is it exactly that He is going to do when He does do something? Over the years, I have forfeited my peace, rest, and joy by not trusting that at the end of the day, He is going to sort things out for me and make sure I get where I should be and doing what I should be doing. Giving my life to God is living by faith and by definition is called trust.

Webster's Dictionary defines trust as: Basic dependence on someone or something; belief that something will happen, or someone will act in a prescribed way. The Bible describes how God will move and act in our lives on every page. Every story that we read in the Bible is there to encourage us that whatever good God did for that person, He will do for us. That is why the story is there. It is to encourage us in our walk of faith that God truly is no respecter of persons and what He did all of those thousands of years ago, He is willing and able to do for us.

He Is Faithful

When we read that God *was* faithful, God is reminding us, He *is* faithful. The same is true of His power, provision and purpose. Whatever we need, He gave us His Word that He will act in a prescribed way. The Bible was written to tell us how God feels about us and how He longs to take care of us. James 1:17 also reminds us that the God we serve does not sleep nor slumber, and every good and perfect gift comes from Him, the Father of lights, with whom there is no variableness, or changing, nor shadow of turning. God is always ready to do something powerful. He is ready to move and bless us when we trust Him.

One of my favorite Scriptures in the Bible is Numbers 23:19. In the late 90's, that passage of Scripture became very personal to me when my dad was diagnosed with lymphoma cancer. He was already in the hospital when my family called me, the youngest of five children, and told me the diagnosis. Out of my spirit came these words, "The next seven years of his life will be his greatest years ever."

After I received the call, I went to stay with him in the hospital. After several days of being in the room with him, one afternoon, while he napped, I was resting with my eyes closed. All of a sudden, I saw a large, lethargic frog in my mind's eye. At first I thought it was some kind of psychotic reaction from being in the hospital too long, but something inside of me said, "Curse cancer." I stood up in that room and said, "I curse the spirit of cancer in Jesus' name." Five minutes later my dad woke up from a sound sleep and called me to his bedside. He said, "Kent, I just had a strange dream." I asked, "What was it, Daddy?" He said, "I dreamed I was throwing up frog legs. I believe it has something to do with this cancer."

Well, as you can only imagine my faith went right through the ceiling. I knew God was doing something for my dad. He had a tumor in his abdomen that was inoperable. So they started chemotherapy and did one round. I left knowing God was moving powerfully in his life.

I went home two days later, and had no sooner gotten home from the airport when my sisters called me to rush back because the doctors had told them my dad was about to die. I said, "That is impossible." They said, "It is not the cancer. He has caught a staph infection in the hospital and because of it we almost lost him." I rushed back to the hospital to my dad's bedside. It was life or death for a while.

I was sitting next to his bed, and I said, "God, You said to me that the next seven years of his life were going to be the greatest years ever. God, please, what is this? I know You did not lie to me." And just like that, I opened my Bible to His response.

As I opened my Bible, I realized what portion of Scripture was before me. Numbers 23:19 states, "God is not a man that He can lie, nor a son of man that He should change His mind. Has He said it, will He not do it? Has He spoken it, will He not make it good?" I left that hospital knowing that God was going to do what He said He was going to do. As I look back on it now, I see the hand of God at every juncture while my dad battled that deadly disease and staph infection.

Ultimately, God received all of the glory because my dad was only able to take one chemo treatment because of the staph infection even though he was scheduled for several treatments. He went back to the doctor four weeks later. Not only had he been healed of the staph infection, but they could not find a trace of cancer in his body anywhere. God does not lie. If God told you something, you can count on Him. He will do it if you will trust Him.

Most of us never get to enter that restful place of trusting God because we do not believe Him. We do not believe His Word. We lean on our own understanding. We trust His Word part of the time and lean on our own understanding the rest of the time. Because of doubt and fear, we never enter into His promised rest.

Hebrews 4:1-3 is a very powerful portion of Scripture. "Therefore, since the promise remains of entering His rest, let us fear, lest any of you seem to come short of it. For indeed, the gospel was preached unto us, as well as unto them, but the word which they heard did not profit them, not being mixed with faith in those who heard it. For we who have believed do enter into that rest, as He said, 'For I have sworn in my wrath, they shall not enter my rest,' although the works were finished from the foundations of the world. "

God is telling us, "I have already done what I had to do in order to bless your life and get you where you are supposed to be." These works were done from the foundation of the earth. God planned our destiny and direction before we were ever born. Psalm 139:16 assures us that while we were yet in our mother's womb, He formed us and our days, fashioned them, and had a plan for our lives that we could walk in if we would trust and surrender our lives to Him. He will begin to direct our paths and it will become a time of rest. We will find rest when we are able to completely trust in God, believing that He will do what He said He would do.

Many of us do not believe God is really in control. We trust ourselves but sooner or later God will allow circumstances to prevail that we cannot get ourselves out of. It may be physical, financial, emotional, marital, or relational, but no matter what the situation is, it will be such that we have to completely trust God for the solution and we will not be able to lean on our own understanding. The really good news is that when we find ourselves in that situation, we have a trustworthy God that we can count on.

Daddy Is On Deck

Recently, I read about an incident in the life of a famous sea captain during the days of the great sailing vessels. He was crossing the Atlantic from Liverpool to New York when his ship ran into a fierce storm. The waves were gigantic. The wind blew with hurricane force and the ship was violently tossed about. The passengers were terror stricken, pulling on their life vests, and preparing for the worst.

The captain's eight-year-old daughter was aboard that trip and was awakened by the noise. She cried out in alarm, asking what was wrong. The crew told her of the storm and the perilous condition of the ship. She asked this question, "Is my father on deck?" They assured her that he was. She smiled a great big smile, laid her head back on the pillow, and was asleep in a matter of minutes. She knew that as long as her daddy was on deck, as captain of that ship, someway, somehow, they were going to make it to the other side. She did not have anything to do with it; she trusted that her father had the capability, the wisdom, and the power, because he had proven to her, in the past, that he was trustworthy. How much more can we trust our heavenly Father to get us out of life's storms? As long as Daddy is at the helm, everything is going to be all right.

In the Amplified version of the Bible Hebrews 13:5 speaks to us so clearly, "For He, God, Himself has said, and the statement is on record, 'I will not, I will not, I will not, in any degree, leave you helpless, nor forsake you, nor let you down, nor relax my hold on you.' " God said that and the statement is recorded. In other words, He put it in writing. He said three times, "I will not, in any degree forsake you, nor put you down, nor relax my hold on you." Do you know what that has meant for my life and can mean for yours? We are not holding on to Him, He is holding on to us.

There have been so many times I have gotten into circumstances and believed I had let go of God. I have felt as though my faith had died, trust in God had left, peace and rest had vanished. I have felt as though my faith and trust was in direct correlation to how faithful I have been. Like you, I am in the process and still learning that what God does is not based on whether I have been good or bad. When things don't happen on the time line I believe they should, it is my lack of capacity to sustain it that is the hold up. The good news is that God gives me another opportunity to grow and mature. God's timing is not mine and that is one lesson I have learned well.

It is during these times of my capacity being enlarged that I encourage myself in the Lord just as David did at Ziklag in I Samuel 30. I remind myself that when I am faithless, He is faithful. When I am weak, He is strong. When I feel as though I cannot go on, He is there to cheer me on to the finish line. That is the one thing I have purposed in my heart. I may grow weary, I may not be full of faith at all times, but I will rejoice in the Lord always and I will finish the course that He has set before me. Is that because I believe in myself? The exact opposite of that is the answer. It is because I believe in God, Who is in complete control of my life. As long as I seek His will for my life, I cannot get off track. I may make some detours along the way, but His Word promises that He rewards those who diligently seek Him and I desire to be numbered among those.

When our children were little, I didn't trust that they would hold onto me when we were crossing a busy intersection. I would grab them by the arm and basically drag them across to make sure they got where we were supposed to go. I have good news for you, if you feel like your grip on God has loosened, be encouraged. You are not holding Him, He is holding you. He will make sure that we get where we are supposed to and that the detours in our lives ultimately place us in the direction we were supposed to be heading all along.

We can trust this God that we serve. The trusting part is not usually the problem. My problem, and it may be yours as well, is always going back to my own understanding. I cannot stop trying to figure God out in my mind. That is why it is called faith. We have to trust that His Word is true and that His promises are for us.

Romans 8:7 clarifies why our reasoning isn't reliable, "The carnal mind is at enmity with God." The Bible reminds us in I Corinthians 2:9 that our flesh will never be able to comprehend spiritual things. "Eye has not seen, ear has not heard, the mind cannot comprehend the good things God has for us, because they are revealed by the Spirit." We can never figure God out intellectually. Scholars and theologians have tried for thousands of years, but it will never happen. Our flesh simply is not designed to know spiritual things as it is our spirit that He reveals Himself to. The Spirit of God reveals things to us in part. My theory is that if we knew more than God revealed, it would be too much for our clay vessels to contain.

The parable in Luke 16: 20-27 about a rich man who died and went to hell comes to mind. When he arrived in hell, he could see across a vast gulf that was between him, and the others and he said, "Please just let somebody go back from the dead and tell my brothers that it is really true." God responded that even if He let somebody from the dead go back, they still would not believe. He said if they have not believed My Word, they will not even believe someone back from the dead. Why do you think God responded in such a way? When you start trying to prove something, people just want more proof. It is an issue of faith. Without faith we cannot become followers of Christ. Faith is a gift from God and comes from God. That is why it is so powerful. He gives us the gift to trust Him as long as we will not lean unto our own understanding.

Be Encouraged

The chapter of Genesis fifteen always encourages me. When I read about men of God who failed I realize that I am not the only one who blows it. I love the failures in the Bible. They encourage me greatly in God because I have failed many times and know that as long as I am alive I will continue to make mistakes. I am especially encouraged when I read about the life of Abraham. He was a man who left his home and went to an unknown country to follow and serve God. God appeared to him three times, in physical form, yet Abraham still doubted Him. It encourages me that somebody that God *appeared to* would still doubt Him. It is encouraging to know that even Abraham, the Father of Faith, would become so afraid at a point in his life that he was ready to give his wife to another man, not once, but twice, because he was afraid he was going to be killed. Call me crazy, but that encourages me. If his faith was tried and he failed, yet God could still do something through him, then I know God has not given up on me.

What did God say to Abraham? "After these things, the word of the Lord came to Abraham in a vision, saying, 'Do not be afraid, Abram. I am your shield, your exceeding great reward.'" If Abraham had not been afraid God would not have said, "Do not be afraid." Abraham was going through a very difficult time and he was afraid. God said, "Do not be afraid. I am your shield and exceeding great reward. " "But," Abraham asked, "Lord God, what will You give me, seeing I go childless?" Abraham was asking, "God, how will You do something in my life, seeing the natural circumstances, that my wife is barren, my body is old, there is no way it can happen in the natural. What are You going to do for me *seeing* the circumstances and the situation?"

Many of us face the same thing. God has already told us in Phillipians 4:19 what His plan is, "I will supply all your needs according to My riches in glory by Christ Jesus." We ask, "Lord, how will You do that *seeing* I have been laid off, I do not have a job, my bills are piled up, people I owe money to are knocking on the door. How will You provide for me, seeing my circumstances?" Yet through His Word, He assures us we are going to live, prosper, and be in good health. The reality may be that you are asking, "Lord, how can You do that? Sickness is manifesting in my body and the pain is relentless." The life stories are as endless as are the questions, "How will my son be saved, seeing he is a drug addict, my daughter is bi-polar and my grandchildren profess to be atheists, how will You do something for me, seeing these things?"

Go Outside of Your Tent

God did not tell Abraham He was going to do anything miraculous. God just said, "Hey, Abraham, get outside your tent." What was He saying? He was saying just walk away from your circumstances for a minute. Quit focusing on your circumstances and start focusing on Me and what I have told you. Lift your eyes up to heaven and count the stars. That is the number of your children. When I first read that portion of Scripture I was living in Florida so I went outside and looked up and there were three stars in the night sky. I thought, "Well, that was not very cool."

Have you ever done that? Put something to the test that you have read in the Bible and like me, you look and there are only about three stars in the night sky? Then I had the opportunity to visit Mount Sinai on a mission's trip. Because there is no ambient light to block the stars you can see millions upon millions of stars with the naked eye. Actually, the sky is full of stars at all times, we just cannot see them when the sun is out or when city lights block them.

Abraham saw millions of stars. God said, "You see in the natural that you do not have a child, but this is what I am going to do. I am going to give you millions of them." Abraham received a lesson in faith that is relevant to all of us right now. Faith sees the invisible, believes the incredible, and receives the impossible. It is time we stop looking at what we are seeing with our natural eyes and begin to look by faith, with our spiritual eyes, at what God is showing us. The things we see in the natural are temporary, but what God is doing supernaturally is eternal.

When we stop focusing on our problems and start focusing on Him and His Word, He becomes bigger than our problems. It is then that we can stay focused on the big picture. Many of us have big problems, but God is bigger. We are not holding on to Him, He is holding on to us, so we must stop looking at our circumstances. Remember Genesis 15: 5, "Get out of your tent, lift your eyes up to heaven from whence comes your help. My help comes from the Lord who created heaven and earth. He that keeps me neither sleeps nor slumbers. He will protect me by day from the sun, and by night from the moon. He will preserve my going in and my coming out from this time forth, and forever more." Psalm 121:1 exhorts us to remember Who is really in charge or to ask the question "Who's your Daddy?"

Perfect Love

Love: Unselfish, loyal and benevolent concern for the good of another: as *(1)*: the fatherly concern of God for humankind.

Chapter Five

Having already established the foundation that the fear of the Lord is reverential, not terror driven, let's take a moment to explore the concept of the fear of the Lord as a very important principle for good success. Proverbs 3:7-8 tells us, "Do not be wise in your own eyes. Fear the Lord, depart from evil. It will be health to your flesh and strength to your bones." The Amplified Bible does just that, it amplifies the same Scripture, "Be not wise in your own eyes, reverently fear and worship the Lord, turn entirely away from evil. It shall be health to your nerves and sinews and marrow and moistening to your bones."

If we were truthful, we could all say it would be wonderful to have peace for our nerves and health in all of our bodily parts. Marrow is the substance of our spinal cord, the innermost, best, or essential part. Bone marrow, moistened with His Presence, His Word, and His life can be nothing but life-giving. Fearing God is one of the most important keys because it has to do with our innermost or essential being, our best or most essential part.

"Do not be wise in your own eyes…" speaks of being prideful, haughty, or puffed up. Believing that our own might or power has gotten us where we are is being wise in our own eyes. Trusting in something other than God, perhaps in finances or a career, is being wise in our own eyes. Trusting in position, lineage, or in anything but God diminishes what God has done in our lives because we believe it is our position that put us on the receiving end of being blessed when, in fact, it was God Who positioned us to receive.

The older I get, the more I realize how little I know. It would seem that the older we get the more we would know but it is just the opposite. If we are really honest we can admit that age does not increase our knowledge and we really do not know as much as we thought that we did. That is especially true concerning the Word of God. When I first became a follower of Christ I thought I knew God. Yet the more of

His Word I read, the more I realized I hardly knew Him at all. Not that I wasn't on a quest and that I didn't know a bit about Him, but in reality He is so vast even if we were all spiritual giants, which most of us are not, we could only comprehend but so much about God.

In Psalm 131:1 David said this pretty well, "Lord, my heart is not haughty, nor my eyes lofty. Neither do I concern myself with great matters, nor with things too profound for me." That is a very interesting portion of Scripture to me because at various times in my life I have gotten involved in conversations I knew absolutely nothing about and tried to act like I knew something that I did not. At the end of the day that becomes really embarrassing.

I have finally come to a point in my life that I am enjoying the great luxury of not having to impress anyone. I do not feel compelled to give an answer that I simply do not have. How liberating it is to say, "I do not know the answer." It is especially freeing when the question on the table is a deeply theological one and I really do not have a clue because it is not something God has revealed to me nor asked me to research.

I take my cue from David who had learned a key about God. He learned to not concern himself with matters that were too high for him. He learned something very important. In Psalm 131: 1-3 he said, "My heart is not haughty, my eyes are not lofty (this denotes pride and arrogance). I do not concern myself with great matters, nor with things too profound for me." In other words, David was not wise in his own eyes. That is exactly why he had such a reverential fear of the Lord. He knew the Lord had done so much for him and he understood that God held the power of life and death in His hand. That is why the next two verses are so powerful, "Surely I have calmed and quieted my soul, like a weaned child with his mother, like a weaned child is my soul within me." When we stop being arrogant, prideful, and wise in our own eyes, we will literally become like a weaned child. We will become quiet and calm.

One of my favorite Scriptures is Isaiah 30:15, "In quietness and confidence shall be your strength." Learning to fear and trust the Lord and not concern ourselves with things that are too high for us prevents us from becoming prideful and arrogant. Having the fear of the Lord prepares us for the times in life that we have to humble ourselves and acknowledge that we have to have a relationship with God to make the big decisions. Our wisdom is not going to produce it for us. Our education, training, or wealth will not get it for us. There will come a time when we will have to acknowledge God.

Lester Sumrall once said, "Life is humbling. You have to have help coming in and you have to have help going out. Everything in between can be very humbling." Life is humbling and that is why when we are humbled, we begin to understand the fear of the Lord. The fear of the Lord is the beginning of wisdom. A fool is the one that says, "There is no God." Outside of the fear of God, there is no wisdom.

Every time I have become involved in matters that I took upon myself and God did not specifically speak to me about I have failed, then condemned myself for that failure. I found this interesting Scripture in Luke 21:26: "In the end times there are going to be signs in the sun and the moon and the stars and on earth distress of nations, perplexity, the sea and the waves roaring and earthquakes, rumors of wars and men's hearts failing them from fear and the expectation of those things which are coming on the earth. For the powers of the heavens will be shaken." Any expectation I have ever had from any source other than God had the potential to fail.

In our society and culture it is wisdom from God that will sustain us and cause us to succeed. Luke 21:7-18 has already come to pass in our lifetime. Who would have thought we would experience 9/11? Who would have thought that the stock market would have become so volatile in recent years, or that terrible diseases for which man cannot find a cure would continue to prevail in such an advanced technological age, or that terrorism would be encroaching?

The Bible has prepared those who are reading it that circumstances are going to get worse. The Word of God tells us very pointedly that in the end times things as we know them are going to get so bad that men's hearts are going to fail from fear. Frankly, that has been happening for years. Heart disease is at an all time high and it has been medically proven that it is because of anxiety, fear, and stress. Men's hearts are literally failing while they are trying to figure out how they are going to survive and how they are going to provide for their families. So many men and women never take into account the wisdom or counsel of God.

We have to get back to the fear of the Lord. Oswald Chambers wrote, "The remarkable thing about fearing God is that when you fear God you do not fear anything else, whereas if you do not fear God, you fear everything else." David was humbled by the fear of the Lord and he enjoyed a restful, quiet, peace that came from his reverence for a Holy God.

What is the Fear of the Lord?

What is the fear of the Lord? It is the opposite of self-dependence, self-confidence, and pride. Fear does not mean being afraid as the English definition would describe it. It is not fear, foreboding, or apprehension or the kind of fear that brings torment. God told us very clearly in 2 Timothy 1:7 that He has not given us the spirit of fear, but of power, love and a sound mind. Even on Judgment Day Christians should not have fear that terrorizes or fear that torments. Our fear is reverential and respectful.

I John 4:16-18 states, "If we have known and believed the love God has for us and that God is love and He that dwells in love dwells in God and God in him herein is our love made perfect that we may have boldness in the Day of Judgment because as He is so are we in the world. There is no fear in love but perfect love cast out all fear." There is nothing about the fear of God that is associated with terror or suspicion.

The fear the Bible teaches is reverence, awe, and worship. It teaches us about respect and reverence. There is fear but it is not the fear of something bad. It is a holy reverence God wants us to have for Him. Luke 12:1-9 explains, "In the meantime, when an innumerable multitude of people had gathered together, so that they trampled one another, He began to say to His disciples first of all, 'Beware of the leaven of the Pharisees, which is hypocrisy. For there is nothing covered that will not be revealed, nor hidden that will not be known. Therefore, whatever you have spoken in the dark will be heard in the light, and what you have spoken in the ear in the inner rooms will be proclaimed on the housetops."

Luke 12: 5 is enough to make me fear and respect a holy God, "And I say unto you, My friends, do not be afraid of those that kill the body, and after that they have no more that they can do. But I will show you whom you should fear: Fear Him that after He has killed, has power to cast into hell. Yes, I say unto you, fear Him."

It is not God's desire for us to be separated from Him eternally which is my understanding of hell. John 3:16 is crystal clear about God's plan for mankind, "God so loved *the world*, He gave His only begotten Son, that whosoever believed in Him would not perish, but have everlasting life."

Stop putting Him in second, third, and last place and start putting Him first. Malachai 1:8 begs the question, "If you treated your governor this way, would he be favorable to you?" Stop giving Him your prayer time when you are exhausted, have done everything else during the day, and then try to worship Him right before you go to bed and offer some lay me down before I sleep, pray the Lord my soul to keep, God bless me, amen prayer, snore, snore.

Before you buy your bass boat or new golf clubs, do something for Him and His kingdom. Do not give Him leftovers. God has no problem with golf clubs and bass boats, and He has no problem with praying before going to sleep at night, but He is saying, "Honor, respect and love Me. If it were not for Him, we would not be here.

My wife and I are in covenant with God and our first payment each month goes to Him to build the Kingdom. We want to honor Him first, above all else, and for Him to know, by our first fruits, that we love, honor, and are obedient to Him. What if the President of the United States showed up in your hometown? What would that be like? Well my goodness, there would be so many special provisions made and everything would be just right. We would all be dressed up, everybody would be on their best behavior, and when he got to the door and they announced, "The President of the United States," we would be up on our feet. Military personnel would be giving him a salute and we would applaud him. He holds the highest office in the land, because he is the President of the United States. How much more should we honor and reverence the Kings of kings and the Lord of lords?

The Fear of the Lord is the Beginning of Wisdom

Once again we come right back to what really is the point of all of it. Why did God, the Creator of the Universe, put all of this in place? The answer is found in Psalm 112:1, "Praise the Lord! Blessed is the man who fears the Lord." The best way to understand what it means to fear the Lord is to discover what people are like who fear the Lord. Proverbs 1:7 reminds us, "The fear of the Lord is the beginning of knowledge, but fools despise wisdom and instruction." Proverbs 9:10 declares, "The fear of the Lord is the beginning of wisdom and the knowledge of the Holy One is understanding." Proverbs 15:33 continues in this same vein, "The fear of the Lord is the instruction of wisdom and before honor is humility." Psalm 111:10 continues this revelation, "The fear of the Lord is the beginning of wisdom." When anyone really learns to fear the Lord, his whole manner of life is affected. Proverbs 16:6 brings it home, "By mercy and truth, iniquity is purged and by the fear of the Lord men depart from evil."

Several years ago I had the opportunity to teach at a rehab center with sixty recovering addicts in attendance. Most of them were there for the second and third time. When I was delivered from drugs I never went back. I never went to rehab nor did I ever have a taste for or even a desire to do them again, so I was really stuck as to why these men just did not seem able to break free of the bondage of addiction. I asked God why I was so completely delivered and so many are not? I know that God is no respecter of persons and that He does not love me any more than He does anyone else, so it made sense to me that He would deliver everybody that wanted to be free in the same way. I asked, "God, why is it these men are not free from addiction, why is it some never go back and some do?" The Lord answered immediately and said, "Kent, they do not understand the fear of the Lord." I understood immediately.

Proverbs 16:6 tells us that by mercy and truth iniquity is taken away, but by the fear of the Lord you depart from it. If you have a healthy fear and respect for God it will cause you to run from evil. You will not be lured by adultery, pride, or covetousness. When someone learns to fear the Lord his whole manner of life is affected. It becomes apparent by the way he dresses, talks, spends his money, spends his time, what he hears, the places he goes, the pleasures he seeks, and even the books he reads. Malachi 3:16 gives a great model for us to emulate, "Then they that fear the Lord spoke often one to another."

Real fear of God is not only about honoring and worshipping Him, it is for our admonition. Proverbs 14:26 says, "In the fear of the Lord is strong confidence, and His children shall have a place of refuge." We all want our children to have a place of refuge. Proverbs 19:23 continues, "The fear of the Lord tends to life and he that has it shall abide satisfied. He shall not be visited with evil." What a promise that is. Ecclesiastes 8:12-13 elaborates, "Though a sinner do evil a hundred times and his days be prolonged, yet surely I know it shall be well with them that fear God, which fear before Him. But it shall not be well with the wicked, neither shall be prolonged days which are a shadow because he fears not before God."

Even when we fear and love God, and are walking in the admonition of the Lord, we may still be working next to or living beside someone that does not fear God at all. The man or woman that does not fear God may appear to have no problems while we seemingly have all of the trials. Deuteronomy 28:13 is clear that at the end of the day those that fear the Lord are going to be the head and not the tail.

Asaph said it like this in Psalm 73:1-28, "Truly God *is* good to Israel, to such as are pure in heart. But as for me, my feet had almost stumbled; my steps had nearly slipped for I *was* envious of the boastful, when I saw the prosperity of the wicked. For *there are* no pangs in their death, but their strength *is* firm. They *are* not in trouble *as other* men, nor are they plagued like *other* men. Therefore pride serves as their necklace; Violence covers them *like* a garment. Their eyes bulge with abundance; they have more than heart could wish. They scoff and speak wickedly *concerning* oppression; they speak loftily. They set their mouth against the heavens, and their tongue walks through the earth. Therefore his people return here, and waters of a full *cup* are drained by them. And they say, "How does God know? And is there knowledge in the Most High?" Behold, these *are* the ungodly, who are always at ease; they increase *in* riches. Surely I have cleansed my heart *in* vain, and washed my hands in innocence. For all day long I have been plagued, and chastened every morning. If I had said, "I will speak thus," Behold, I would have been untrue to the generation of Your children. When I thought *how* to understand this, it *was* too painful for me, until I went into the sanctuary of God; *then* I understood their end. Surely You set them in slippery places; You cast them down to destruction. Oh, how they are *brought* to desolation, as in a moment! They are utterly consumed with terrors. As a dream when *one* awakes, s*o,* Lord, when You awake, You shall despise their image. Thus my heart was grieved, and I was vexed in my mind. I *was* so foolish and ignorant; I was *like* a beast before You. Nevertheless I *am* continually with You; You hold *me* by my right hand. You will guide me with Your counsel, and afterward receive me *to* glory. Whom have I in heaven *but You.* And *there is* none upon earth *that* I desire besides You. My flesh and my heart fail; b*ut* God *is* the strength of my heart and my portion forever. For indeed, those who are far from You shall perish; You have destroyed all those who desert You for harlotry. But *it is* good for me to draw near to God; I have put my trust in the Lord God, that I may declare all Your works." Asaph came to the conclusion that the end is better than the beginning for those who fear God.

Confidence is won in God because the one who fears God lives in very intimate and personal communion with the Lord. Psalm 25:12-14 expresses a powerful statement about the fear of the Lord. "Who is the man that fears the Lord? Him shall He teach in the way that He chooses. He himself shall dwell in prosperity, and his descendants shall inherit the earth. The secret of the Lord is with those who fear Him, and He will show Him His covenant." Number one, God is going to direct you in the way that He chooses if you fear Him. Number two, you are going to dwell in prosperity. Number three, your descendants are going to inherit the earth. Number four, the secret of the Lord is going to be with you, and number five, He is going to show you His covenant. All of these blessings are ours when we reverently fear and honor the Lord.

We Really are Friends of God

We all want to have direction in our lives. Prosperity is also a desire. And, of course, we want our children to be blessed. For those of us who desire to know and understand the things of God, anything God shares with us is a thrill. God asked, "Would I hide anything from my friend Abraham?"

Like Abraham, we are friends of God and He desires to share His heart and mysteries with us. Abraham feared and respected God with a holy fear and God knew it. God said, "Abraham fears Me and I know that he will cause his house to serve Me." How would you like to be so close to God that He shares His secrets with you?

God wants that kind of relationship with us, His friends. He will not do anything until He reveals it to His prophets and His servants. Who does God share secrets with? He shares secrets with those He can trust. How many of us share secrets with people we cannot trust? Well, we would not do that on purpose anyway. If we did, it would not be a secret much longer would it? Sometimes God will share a secret with us for prayer. God is looking for faithful people who will not jump up and say, "Hey! God showed me this amazing revelation, but it is for the future." Instead, they get on their knees, start praying, and bring that truth to earth for Him.

Those that fear God enjoy a very intimate relationship with Him. Moses talked to God face-to-face, mouth-to-mouth, like a friend talks to another friend. David had an intimate relationship because he listened to God with reverential fear and trembling. Paul had an intimate relationship with God because he experienced God's power firsthand on the road to Damascus when God demanded his attention. Paul responded out of very healthy fear of the Lord. He had been massacring Christians thinking he had been doing God a favor. Trust me, once he heard from God he most certainly had a few anxious moments about the turn his life was about to take.

The most important blessing the fear of God brings is intimacy. As we demonstrate respect, reverence, and live in relationship we become intimate with Him. David was not perfect, but he had a heart after God. He feared, respected, and was in awe of God. God trusts those that fear and revere Him, and He is intimate with them as friends.

I had one of those weeks a while back that I missed the mark and did not do everything I was supposed to do. When I prayed and expressed my love for Him, I expected Him to say something like, "Go, and sin no more." I was praying when all of a sudden I heard the most overwhelming word. Overwhelming because I knew I had not gotten everything just right that week. As I was sitting there in the Presence of God, He spoke these words, "Kent, I trust you." It broke my heart because I thought, "God, You trust me even though You know me and know that I still make a mess of things. That means You must be doing something very powerful in my life to make me trustworthy because I know I am not." The fear of the Lord will cause God to trust, be intimate with, and speak to our hearts in a very powerful way.

I want God to be able to trust me and I want Him to share His secrets with me. I do not want God to come to me when I am out of line. I want God to come by and say, "Hey Kent, I love you so much. Here are a few things that are about to happen in the earth and I wanted to run them by you and see what you think." Don't we all want that kind of intimacy with God? According to Psalm 34: 7-9, protection is found, in the fear of the Lord. "The angel of the Lord encamps around about them that fear Him and delivers them. Oh fear the Lord you saints, for there is no want to those who fear Him." The fear of the Lord has to be chosen states Proverbs 1:29-30, "For they hated knowledge and did not choose the fear of the Lord." We have a choice.

When we choose to live a life of godly fear, we learn to revere a holy God. Deuteronomy 4:10 directs us to, "Gather Me the people together and I will make them hear My words, that they may learn to fear Me." Psalm 34:11 elaborates, "Come you children, hearken unto Me. I will teach you the fear of the Lord." Then Nehemiah 1:11 continues, "Oh, Lord I beseech You, let now Your ear be attentive to the prayer of Your servant and to the prayer of Your servants who desire to fear Your name and prosper."

The Book of Remembrance

Malachi 3:16-18 and 4:1-2 hold the most powerful promise for the destination of those who fear God, "Then those who feared the Lord spoke to one another, and the Lord listened and He heard them. So a book of Remembrance was written before Him for those that fear the Lord and meditate on His name. 'They shall be Mine,' says the Lord of hosts. 'On the day that I make up My jewels, I will spare them as a man spares his own son who serves him.' Then you shall again discern between the righteous and the wicked, between he who serves God and the one who does not serve Him. For behold the day is coming, burning like an oven and all the proud, yes all who do wickedly shall stumble. And the day which is coming shall burn them up, says the Lord of hosts. That will leave them neither root nor branch. But to you who fear My name, the Son of Righteousness shall arise with healing in His wings."

I pray that the spirit of the fear of the Lord will live within you. Adhere to the counsel of Proverbs 3:7-8, "Be not wise in your own eyes, but fear the Lord, depart from evil. It will be health to your flesh and strength to you bones" Desire a deeper understanding with more of the spirit of the fear of the Lord, and you too will begin to burn with a passion to live a godly, good success filled life before a holy God.

Money, Money, Money

Money: Something generally accepted as a medium of exchange, a measure of value, or a means of payment.

Chapter Six

Do you remember the song by the O 'Jays *For the Love of Money*? It starts out *"Money, Money, Money,"* and then the verse is, *"For the love of money I need—I need. For the love of money keep me happy, don't let money rule ya—don't let money fool you, no."* While writing this chapter, I was reminded of that old song and thought how, too often, even in the church we find ourselves being ruled and fooled by the love of money.

In Matthew, Mark, Luke and John Jesus either mentions or refers to money twenty-five times. Wealth and treaures are other topics that become object lessons not only for the disciples but for us as well. Jesus did speak about wealth but there was always a central theme and it is east and west from what culture and the world system describes and dictates. Yet, He did focus His teachings on money more often than He did Heaven and Hell combined. Seemingly, He was trying to make a point. He taught and used parables about money in eleven out of thirty-nine parables and in the gospel of Luke one out of every seven verses has something for us to learn about money.

Jesus did talk about money a lot but the point was for us to trust that God's promises are real and that we when we are obedient to follow His plans for our lives we will be blessed and *become* a blessing to others. His teaching was central to Matthew 16:9, "Do not lay up for yourselves treasures on earth, where moth and rust destroy and where thieves break in and steal," and His counsel to the rich, young ruler in Luke 18:22 still rings true, "You still lack one thing. Sell all that you have and distribute to the poor, and you will have treasure in heaven; and come, follow Me." His radical message was to forget everything they had learned while subject to the world system and become subjects of the Kingdom.

Proverbs 3:9 encourages us to, "Honor the Lord with your possessions, and with the first fruits of all your increase..." This principle is the first godly directive that my wife and understood as we began to seek the Kingdom of God first as Matthew 6:33 instructs us to do.

We were not very good stewards when we lived according to culture and the world system. Saving and investing didn't really enter into the equation. When we were first married we called our front door the hundred dollar door because every time one or the other of us went out of it you could count on at least one hundred dollars being spent.

At the time I was making a very good salary and we could afford to do just about anything we wanted to. I was also young, immature and had not even started to consider the future. We both lived in the moment and it was fun, for a little while. The first year that I neglected to pay my income taxes was not really a big deal (in the theater of my mind) I figured I'd catch up the next year. Well, you know how fast time goes so before I knew it I was three years in arrears and my whole life, including my lifestyle, had changed.

The job was gone but the debt from the former lifestyle remained. With penalties and interests my back taxes went from $40,000.00 to $100,00.00. With compounded quarterly interests there was no end in sight. After I became a follower of Christ I decided to call the IRS. After spending a sleepless night tossing, turning and imagining myself in debtor's prison (which thankfully we do not have in the United States of America) I did call and ask what could be done to remedy the situation.

The representative that I spoke to was very accommodating and told me the exact amount that I owed and where to send the check. I respectfully told her that the only problem would be that I did not have $100,00.00 to send. She said that would not be a problem that an IRS agent would be at my house that next Monday morning. Needless to say I tossed and turned quite a bit more between my phone call that Friday and the arrival of said IRS agent Monday.

I had worked myself into quite a state by the time we sat down to discuss a payment plan. In the end every dime that we made beyond paying our bills was garnished. Anything that was of value belonged to the Internal Revenue Service. In reality that was very little as we had already downsized considerably. The one silver lining (looking back I can't help but see God's redemptive power at work) was that we were allowed to tithe. Placing God first in every area of our lives was our goal so it only made sense we would give Him our money first.

We embraced this principle and for the next five years regardless of how dire our circumstance we gave our tithe and offerings to God first.

The guidelines that we find in the Bible about money and how to enjoy the fruit of our labor, or in contemporary terms, the paycheck that comes from accomplishing the work related to whatever fields of endeavor we are pursuing, are really specific. Honoring God with our money is the first concept that we must understand to really begin to live a successful life. Genesis 14:18 describes the Abrahamic covenant and therein is the first time we see the word "tithe," and are introduced to the concept of giving God the first of our income.

This is the story: Abraham is heading back to his home camp after victoriously defeating Chedorlaomer, king of Elam, and was met by the regional king named Melchizedek, who was the priest of the Most High God, to his people. A side note is that considering this was mostly pagan territory, it could not have been happenstance that Abraham met King Melchizedek, whose name is literally translated to mean My King Is Righteous. The priest perceived he was weary from waging war and traveling, so he invited him to join him for a bite of bread and a bit of wine, which at that time must have amounted to a royal banquet. Because Melchizedek welcomed Abraham and shared his provision with him, Abraham in turn, without any legal requirement or provocation, gave him a "tithe" or ten percent of the revenue from the wealth he had brought back from war.

This is not a random encounter that just got thrown into Genesis to take up space. This story is an example of who we are to model our lives after with the revelation that Melchizedek is a shadow or type of Jesus Christ and uniquely held the office of both king and priest, just as we now do as kings and priests unto our God. Abraham was operating in a covenant of grace, not a covenant of the Law. The Abrahamic Covenant is the Old Testament model for the New Covenant that was described in Acts 4:32-35, "And the multitude of them that believed were of one heart and of one soul: neither said any of them that ought of the things which he possessed was his own; but they had all things common. And with great power gave the apostles witness of the resurrection of the Lord Jesus and great grace was upon them all. Neither was there any among them that lacked: for as many as were possessors of lands or houses sold them, and brought the prices of the things that were sold, and laid them down at the apostles' feet: and distribution was made unto every man according as he had need."

Money is Neither Good nor Evil

Many people may believe that tithing is Old Covenant, but it is, in fact, part of the Covenant of Grace. Tithing is not about building buildings and raising money for churches. Tithing is designed to give people an opportunity to come into covenant with God and allow Him to capture our hearts. When we give God our money, it is, just as in ancient times, like sacrificing sheep, lambs, goats, or vegetables. The people were honoring God with what they had produced. As they honored God with their first fruits, they came into covenant with Him, therefore placing themselves into the position of receiving the blessings and promises of the covenant they were upholding. The mentality that money is evil has to be dissimilated and de-mythed once and for all. Money is neither evil nor good.

If you put money in a good man's hand, its purpose will become good. If you put money in an evil man's hand, its purpose will become evil. Money, within and of itself, is neither good nor evil. I Timothy 6:10 explains what the root cause of the problem is: "For the love of money is the root of all evil: which while some coveted after, they have erred from the faith, and pierced themselves through with many sorrows." Money is just money, but tradition and religion have taught us that money is evil. Proverbs 28:19-22 sums it up, "God, never let me have so much that I forget about You and God never let me have too little that I have to steal to eat." That is the balance that allows God to bless our lives.

Abraham is called the Father of Faith because he received from God under grace, not the Law, and came to understand that righteousness, by faith, can also be received. Abraham's revelation is the same understanding of God that we in the 21st century must embrace: to have good success we must trust God with our finances. We must allow Him to minister to us in this area of our lives so that the spirit of poverty and the mentality that accompanies it is defeated and destroyed.

During our years of paying back the IRS we continued to live under God's covenant of grace and even though we didn't exactly prosper financially we were extremely blessed. Frankly, the situation was hopeless had we just looked at it as it was. We were paying the paltry amount of $200.00. a month against a $100,00.00 debt. The interest kept right on compounding quarterly and there was no end in sight. We continued to tithe and give offerings but we were literally enslaved by that massive debt.

Our faith was huge that God would somehow, someway break us out of the choke hold that was on our finances.

In the spring of 1993 we made a decision that completely changed our lives. My wife really believed that God had instructed her to publish a book that would encourage others to be free from the emotional bondage of unforgiveness. Faithfully, she began to write it and in the process realized how deeply entrenched in anger, bitterness and unforgiveness she was. It had been sixteen years since she had seen her imprisoned Father and she knew she had to see him before she would be completely free.

Little did we know the impact that choice would have on our entire family. In obedience we packed up and prepared to make the twelve hour journey. The onslaught from the enemies' camp was immediate and with each obstacle we became more determined to see the trip through.

The visit did not go that well for my wife but the end result was nothing if not miraculous. My wife did begin to develop a real relationship with her Father that ultimately lead to his salvation and two weeks after we saw him we were approached by a man in our church that wanted to help us negotiate with IRS. After a few months of meetings we were able to offer them a settlement which was accepted and literally overnight we were free from a massive debt. The same man who had walked through all of the negotiations blessed us with the $10,000.00 to pay the settlement and the extra $2,000.00 for the taxes to cover it.

It had taken five years but we continued to give faithfully and trust that God would intervene on our behalf. God enlarged our capacities and we were faithful with the little we had. During that time we learned about His character, commission and Kingdom.

The Great Commission

Jesus commissioned us in Matthew 25:31-40 to feed the hungry and clothe the naked: "When the Son of Man comes in His glory, and all the holy angels with Him, then He will sit on the throne of His glory. All the nations will be gathered before Him, and He will separate them one from another, as a shepherd divides his sheep from the goats. And He will set the sheep on His right hand, but the goats on the left. Then the King will say to those on His right hand, 'Come, you blessed of My Father, inherit the kingdom prepared for you from the foundation of the world: for I was hungry and you gave Me food; I was thirsty and you gave Me drink; I was a stranger and you took Me in; I was naked and you clothed Me; I was sick and you visited Me; I was in prison and you came to Me.' Then the righteous will answer Him, saying, 'Lord, when did we see You hungry and feed You, or thirsty and give You drink? When did we see You a stranger and take You in, or naked and clothe You? Or when did we see You sick, or in prison, and come to You?' And the King will answer and say to them, 'Assuredly, I say to you, inasmuch as you did it to one of the least of these My brethren, you did it to Me.'" That is a very clear directive but it begs the question, "How can we feed the hungry and clothe the naked if we are naked and hungry ourselves? The answer is simple, God gave us a great commission and we cannot do it without money.

So, what is money *really* about? If everybody in the Body of Christ did what God told them to do, we would not have to beg for money to accomplish the work of fivefold ministry. The statistics are astounding. This information was gathered by www.generousgiving.org in 2009:

- Giving by Class: The two groups in the United States that give the highest percentages of their income are the poor (those making less than $20,000 per year) and the rich (those making more than $100,000 per year). Middle-class Americans (those making between $40,000 and $100,000 per year) are the smallest percentage givers.

- Few Support the Church: Only one-third to one-half of U.S. church members financially support their churches.

- Religious Donations: More than $60 billion a year is donated to religious nonprofit organizations. The vast bulk of that sum— more than $40 billion annually—goes directly to churches, almost all of it from individuals.

- Pets: In 2007, it is estimated that Americans spent over $40 billion on their pets.

- Weight Loss: It is estimated that by 2010, Americans will have spent over $60 billion on weight-loss programs.

- Giving Is Not a Priority: Christians worldwide had personal income totaling more than $16 trillion in 2007 but gave only two percent, or $370 billion, to Christian causes.

- Donating over Tithing: Overall, only three to five percent of those who donate money to a church tithe (give ten percent of) their incomes.

- Tithing: Nine percent of American "born-again" adults tithed in 2004.

- Then and Now: Giving by North American churchgoers was higher during the Great Depression (Three and a third percent of per capita income in 1933) than it was after a half-century of unprecedented prosperity (Two and a half percent in 2004).

- Sunday Offerings: The average amount of money given by a full or confirmed member of a U.S. Christian church in 2004 was $691.93. This comes to an average of $13.31 per week.

- Income versus Net Worth: Ninety-Six percent of evangelical giving is given out of income, and only four percent is given out of net worth. (Ron Blue & Co.)

- Enormous Prosperity: At the turn of the 21st century, the United States was home to 276 billionaires, over 2,500 households with a net worth exceeding $100 million, 350,000 individuals with a net worth of $10 million, and 5 million millionaires.

- High Wealth, Small Population: Americans own approximately forty percent of the world's wealth but comprise only two and a half percent of the world's population.

- Incomes Up, Giving Down: Incomes have gone up 9 to 10 times in the last 20 years while giving has gone down about fifty percent.

Wow! The wildest part about those statistics is that if Christians just gave the ten percent modeled in the Word, we could *eradicate poverty globally*. There would be enough for everybody and I believe that welfare would be done away with because we would be fulfilling the Great Commission and functioning in our purpose and God's plan for mankind. When we start honoring God the way He put the tithe into place to honor Him, we will undoubtedly begin to experience good success. There are over sixteen hundred verses throughout Scripture that mention money and what to do and not do with it. The most challenging concept about how to handle our funds is the most fundamental. First and foremost, it is not about money. It is about trusting and putting God first concerning our treasures and hearts. Our scriptural reference is really clear on this point according to Matthew 6:21: "For where your treasure is, there your heart will be also."

Abraham's commitment to Melchizedek is the first time we see the tithe being implemented. The word tithe means ten percent and it has a very specific meaning and connotation. Ten percent has always seemed rather random and arbitrary to me. I thought that Abraham was being generous with his recent spoils of war and considered ten percent to be magnanimous in relation to a little bit of bread and wine, even if it was considered to be a royal banquet at the time. However, research proved how often God's character was demonstrated throughout Scripture pertaining to allotments of ten.

In accordance with the numerical evaluation assigned to the number ten, I quickly learned that it always speaks of redemption. As examples, there were ten camels sent for Isaac's wife Rebecca, ten donkeys were sent to bring Jacob to Egypt, ten plagues were used to free the Israelites from Egypt, Ten Commandments were given for the Israelites to obey for redemption, and ten days were spent in the upper room before the

Spirit of God fell. Ten is a redemptive number in the Bible. When we give God the tenth, God redeems the ninety and removes the curse that went into effect when Adam fell from grace in the Garden in Genesis 3:17-19: "Cursed is the ground for your sake; In toil you shall eat *of* it all the days of your life. Both thorns and thistles it shall bring forth for you, and you shall eat the herb of the field. In the sweat of your face you shall eat bread till you return to the ground, for out of it you were taken; for dust you are, and to dust you shall return."

Giving God ten percent allows Him to put His hand on the other ninety percent of our income and redeem it. When we tithe, we are operating with redeemed money, not cursed money. Blessed money is what enables us to do so much with so little. That revelation changed mine and my wife's life. Our lifestyle choices before Christ had negated the blessings of God and our minds had to be renewed with the understanding of the difference between living according to the world system and how it operates, and living with a kingdom mentality based on the principles and promises of God.

Proverbs Chapter Three

The basis for this book is the foundational truth found in the book of Proverbs Chapter Three. This chapter is loaded with the wisdom and knowledge of God's character that it takes for us to live a blessed, successful life as believers. As I have studied it, I have come to believe that if we only had Proverbs Chapter Three, we could live a strong Christian life.

Let's take a look at how this principle works and how it can radically change the way we look at our finances. Proverbs 3:1-6 encourages us to remember God and that His commandments and blessings are ours, "My son do not forget my law, but let your heart keep my commands; for length of days and long life and peace they will add to you. Let not mercy and truth forsake you; Bind them around your neck, write them on the tablet of your heart and so find favor and high esteem in the sight of God and man. Trust in the Lord with all your heart, and lean not on your own understanding. In all your ways acknowledge Him, and He shall direct your paths."

The very first verse states that God's success will bring length of days, long life, and peace. The next verse admonishes us to not let mercy and truth forsake us, but to bind them around our neck and we will find favor and high esteem. Favor with God is indeed a blessing. The third verse is about trust. Trusting in the Lord with all your heart and not leaning to your own understanding takes all of the pressure off of us.

Fourth, we are not to be wise in our own eyes (pride), but fear the Lord. Proverbs 3:9-10 continues to encourage us, "Honor the Lord with your possessions and with the first fruits of all your increase, so your barns will be filled with plenty and your vats will overflow with new wine." God's promise to His people is that if we will honor Him, recognizing Him as our source of all blessing, and come into covenant with Him that we will enjoy an abundance of everything in our life. In John 10:10 Jesus said, "I have come that you might have life and have it more abundantly." God's plan from the foundation of the earth was for us to live in His blessings and enjoy abundance.

Abundance does not necessarily imply being rich, driving expensive cars, and living in million dollar homes. If you can afford to do that, it is fine. However, that is not what God is talking about. God told Abraham that He would bless him and make him a blessing. God is not interested in greed, but He is interested in meeting the hierarchy of needs that we all have as humans. He wants us blessed so that all of our bills are paid and our needs are met, but He also wants us to be able to give out of our abundance so that we can help meet someone else's need.

That has been God's plan from the foundation of the earth, but religion and tradition have taught us the opposite. Man-made commandments have taught us that we are supposed to be broke and miserable and because we are broke and miserable we will be humble. Well, believe me I have been broke and miserable and all I got out of it was being broke and miserable.

What is that old saying? Money will not buy you happiness but it will sure make you miserable in a better part of town. Ninety percent of the people I talk to, when you trace their problems: stress, marital issues, and everything else, it goes back to money. Godly finance is something that is not taught enough in church. God's intention is not to get our money. God does not need our money. He does not want our money, He wants our hearts. Matthew 6:21 points out that, "Where your treasure is there will your heart be also." God is not after our money, He is after our hearts.

Living in humility really has nothing to do with how much money we do or do not have. Actually, piety and pride are often tied together when works are believed to produce righteousness. Tradition and religious misperceptions and mindsets have tied a spirit of poverty to godliness which completely negates the blessings of God in our finances. Godly finance is about coming into covenant with God, living according to His Word, and allowing God to manifest Himself in our lives as we honor Him with our possessions and our first fruits.

Humility is not produced by our circumstances. Being down on our luck is not true humility. Circumstances can produce humility but it might not necessarily be spiritual humility. A beggar on the side of the road may act humble and behave as if he has humility, but his true demeanor may be hidden simply because of circumstances. On the inside he may be really vile and reprobate as far as his spiritual life is concerned, yet he has been humbled because of circumstances. True humility is when God has blessed and increased us, yet we remain humble. True humility is when we realize that without God we would not have anything, and we put whatever blessings we have into His hands and allow Him to instruct us as how to best use it for His glory.

The Concept of Firsts

Deuteronomy 26:1-5 explains the concept of firsts, "When you come into the land that I have given you, flowing with milk and honey, bring Me a first fruit." God said, "Give it to Me as an offering or as a tithe and give it to Me in a basket, and take it to the priest and they will offer it up to Me and sacrifice it unto Me. By doing this you are proclaiming Me to be your God and in return I am going to proclaim you to be My people. "

When we honor God, we are not just putting money into the basket to build things. When we tithe we are saying, "You are my God, You are my source, You are my strength. We are trusting that James 1:17 is true, "Every good and perfect gift comes from You, the Father of lights, in whom there is no variableness, nor shadow of turning and I am not trusting my job or my income, I am trusting You." In return, when God sees that kind of faith, He says, "Yes, you are Mine and I will provide for, look after, and protect you. I will guide you because we are in covenant."

There is firstborn, there are first fruits, and there is a first harvest, along with many other firsts in the Bible. We can study it theologically all day long, but here is the layman's interpretation: God wants to be first. That is the bottom line—God wants to be first in our lives. If we will make Him first in our lives our lives will begin to line up with His Word and we will begin to live a blessed life full of good success. When we make Him first with our possessions and our own first fruits, we will see the blessings of God take over our lives.

Deuteronomy 26 depicts the Israelites talking about how God brought them out of Egypt, delivered them, and did great things for them. Then Exodus 34:19-20 and 26 really makes it interesting. It is in this passage that God began to speak to them about first fruits. God said, "The first offering of every womb belongs to Me, including all the firstborn males of your livestock, whether from herd or flock. Redeem the firstborn donkey with a lamb, He said, but if you do not redeem it, break the donkey's neck. For no one is to appear before Me empty-handed. Bring the best of your first fruits from the soil to the house of God."

Leviticus chapter one describes animals that may be sacrificed: "When any one of you brings an offering to the Lord, you shall bring your offering of the livestock—of the herd and of the flock. If his offering *is* a burnt sacrifice of the herd, let him offer a male without blemish; he shall offer it of his own free will at the door of the tabernacle of meeting before the Lord. Then he shall put his hand on the head of the burnt offering, and it will be accepted on his behalf to make atonement for him. He shall kill the bull before the Lord; and the priests, Aaron's sons, shall bring the blood and sprinkle the blood all around on the altar that *is by* the door of the tabernacle of meeting. And he shall skin the burnt offering and cut it into its pieces. The sons of Aaron the priest shall put fire on the altar, and lay the wood in order on the fire. Then the priests, Aaron's sons, shall lay the parts, the head, and the fat in order on the wood that *is* on the fire upon the altar; but he shall wash its entrails and its legs with water. And the priest shall burn all on the altar as a burnt sacrifice, an offering made by fire, a sweet aroma to the Lord. 'If his offering *is* of the flocks—of the sheep or of the goats—as a burnt sacrifice, he shall bring a male without blemish. He shall kill it on the north side of the altar before the Lord; and the priests, Aaron's sons, shall sprinkle its blood all around on the altar. And he shall cut it into its pieces, with its head and its fat; and the priest shall lay them in order on the wood that *is* on the fire upon the altar; but he shall wash the entrails and the legs with water. Then the priest shall bring *it* all and burn *it* on the altar; it *is* a burnt sacrifice, an offering made by fire, a sweet aroma to the Lord. 'And if the burnt sacrifice of his offering to the Lord *is* of birds, then he shall bring his offering of turtledoves or young pigeons. The priest shall bring it to the altar, wring off its head, and burn *it* on the altar; its blood shall be drained out at the side of the altar. And he shall remove its crop with its feathers and cast it beside the altar on the east side, into the place for ashes. Then he shall split it at its wings, *but* shall not divide *it* completely; and the priest shall burn it on the altar, on the wood that *is* on the fire. It *is* a burnt sacrifice, an offering made by fire, a sweet aroma to the Lord."

The clean animals were oxen, goats, sheep, pigeons, and turtledoves. Interestingly enough, in Genesis 15: 9-20 these are the exact animals that Abraham cut covenant with God. God said, "Take the firstborn male of the clean animals and offer it to Me as a devoted thing, the translation being the things devoted to destruction." The first born was devoted to destruction and was to be sacrificed. God said, "If you will do that, I will redeem even the unclean animals of your flock. God said, "If you cannot produce a first fruit to redeem the donkey, it would be better to break its neck and not have the donkey." God was saying, "Unless you are living under My Covenant, with this first fruit principle, it would be better off not even to have the donkey than to have it living under the curse."

When Israel went into the Promised Land they were expecting Paradise. They had been told just as we are in Leviticus 20:24 that it was a land flowing with milk and honey. Milk is produced every day and honey is produced once a year. God was saying that every day and every year I am Jehovah-Jireh, your Provider—I will take care of your needs and provide for you in this land that I am bringing you into.

The first fruit, or the first thing, is devoted to destruction, as a sacrifice. God told them the first city that they would come to was called Jericho. Jericho was a city full of wealth and material blessings, but God said, "Do not touch it, it is the first city." God said, "It is My tithe. You can have all the rest of the land and the rest of the cities, but this city is Mine. It is devoted to destruction." That is why He had them march around the city. He told them to call upon Him and He would destroy the city. God took the first fruit and said, "Do not touch anything."

The Spoils of War

The spoils of war are what are kept for victory. In this battle, the victory was the Lord's and Jericho was devoted as the sacrifice. All of the nation listened and heeded what God had required of them. All, that is, with the exception of one man, Achan, who was from the tribe of Judah. Achan took a little piece of gold out of the spoils, and because he did that, he cursed the whole nation. Joshua 7:1 spells out how it went down, "But the children of Israel committed a trespass regarding the accursed things, for Achan the son of Carmi, the son of Zabdi, the son of Zerah, of the tribe of Judah, took of the accursed things; so the anger of the Lord burned against the children of Israel."

God did not care that he had a little piece of gold. That was not it. It was that he had touched the devoted thing. Could it be that the church is not prospering the way we should because of Achans? Many of us tip God instead of tithing, and we consume the devoted thing for our own pleasures. If it is a good sermon we give Him a good tip, and if it is a bad sermon we give Him a bad tip. God does not want tips, God wants to be first.

Once, while in Holland, I heard this humorless antidote about giving. The currency in Holland is measured in guilders that are gold coins equivalent to the U. S. dollar. As the story goes several men, and boys, were sitting on the front row. When the offering plate was passed one man threw a guilder in. When he got home from the service his wife asked, "How was the service?" He answered, "It was okay. The preacher preached a little bit long." "How was the music?" His response, "Ah, it was ok. It was a bit off-key, but it was alright." "Well, how was the ministry time?" "A few things happened, but not much." His little boy piped up and asked, "Dad, what did you expect for a guilder?"

As we grow in understanding of the principle of first fruit offerings, and begin to live our lives according to the revelation that the first of everything we have belongs to God, there will not be a ministry or a church who is serving God that will struggle financially. God wants His people to be blessed, and as we are obedient to His Word, pertaining to this area of our lives, God is going to continue to pour blessings into the lives of His people and we will begin to live success filled lives.

Discipline is a Love Song?

Discipline: Orderly or prescribed conduct or pattern of behavior.

Chapter Seven

T he title of this chapter may not make much sense to you, but the truth is godly disciplines really do invite not only God's love but also open the door for favor with our fellow humankind. When we realize that God really does chastise and discipline those He loves, and that He is in relationship with those He disciplines, in a weird sort of way discipline becomes another one of His love songs to us, His people. That may seem strange but it is true. Prayerfully, from previous chapters you have a better understanding of how God's mercy and truth leads to favor with God as we trust in the Lord with all our hearts and allow Him to direct our paths. Furthermore, we are learning to not be wise in our own eyes, to fear the Lord and through that process, we have a better understanding that we can live healthy and strong lives, not only spiritually and emotionally, but in our physical bodies as well.

Hopefully, a deepening revelation of honoring the Lord with our possessions so He will fill our barns with plenty and burst our vats with new wine has been imparted as we have learned more about the importance of giving God our first fruits and honoring Him with our increase. When we practice these principles in a systematic way, we begin to see that Proverbs Chapter Three really does have all of the elements we need to mature in our Christian walk.

As we continue to glean from this chapter, there is one portion right in the middle of all these blessings that, as I read it, jumped right off of the page. Proverbs 3:11-12 states, "My son, do not despise the chastening (which means disciplining), of the Lord; nor despise His correction. For whom the Lord loves, He corrects, just as a father, the son in whom he delights." Right in the middle of learning how to have good success, God begins to talk to us about discipline and correction.

I believe if we are going to enjoy a strong life as a believer in the Kingdom of God, we are going to have to learn to not only endure, but also embrace the disciplines of God. Furthermore, we are going to have to learn to not despise it when He corrects us. Admittedly, I do not, as a rule, like to be corrected and I do not like discipline. However, if we are going to enjoy a life of good success, we are going to have to embrace both correction and discipline. Moreover, we have to come to the realization that correction is an act of love, designed to develop our character and to increase our effectiveness for God. When we receive a rebuke, it is because God loves us, not because He hates us. God really does chasten, or discipline, those He loves. You probably already know from experience that it is rarely easy to discipline those we love and are in relationship with. As a matter of fact it is work, hard work if we do it right. It is easier to do whatever task we are trying to teach, or train, someone else to do ourselves, especially when we have to train them to *be* disciplined about performing said task.

Discipline Takes Time

Our own children are great examples of this principle. At our house we are always saying, "Make your bed, make your bed, make your bed, make your bed." The reality is that it is so much easier to make the bed ourselves instead of always explaining why they should make the bed, how to make the bed, and then after they have made it, remake it. That is incredibly time-consuming and frankly, it is annoying and leads to frustration (the frustration being mine and my wife's). It really would be easier to just do it ourselves. Discipline takes time and effort. The reason we discipline our own children is because we love them and because we want them to grow in character and integrity. God is the same way with us. It should show us He loves us when He takes time to discipline us.

Recently, I read a motivational book and this one observation really resonated with me—it is easier to raise boys than deliver men. If we will take time now to discipline our children, prayerfully we will not have to watch them struggle with destructive behaviors later in life. It is the same principle with God. When we embrace His disciplines now, we will not have to be delivered from strongholds later. I have learned that deliverance without discipline is deception. If we think we can come get a zap from God and go on about our business, living any way we want to, we are deceived. If that were true, we would not even have church. We would just have a drive-through. It would be easy, just drive through, get a hit, and keep going. However, that is not the way God does things. It does not happen that way because God is raising a mature army of believers who will proclaim the Good News of the gospel to a lost and dying world.

It makes sense that not all discipline is joyous and pleasurable. Not long ago I saw a picture of a guy with a huge stomach, tight jeans, and no shirt, sitting on a keg of beer. It looked like the seams on his Levi's were about to split, and he was sitting there looking fat and happy. Instead of the caption, "No pain, no gain," this one read, "No pain, no pain." Well, it is true. If there is no pain of discipline in our life, in the end, we may wind up fat, with no shirt, sitting on a keg of beer. Hopefully, that will not be us, but we may wind up in situations and circumstances that we should not be in.

Good Success

To enjoy good success, God wants us to learn how to embrace and endure His chastening. It is all about enduring the process. When God spoke in the book of Genesis, He said something powerful after each created work. The first day He created day and night, and the next He created land and seas. After each creation, He said, "It is good." Here is the point. The first day the process was not over, but He said, "It is good." The second day the process was not over, but He said, "It is good." The third, fourth, and every day that He was not finished, the work was not completed, yet He still said, "It is good." The good news is as long as we are in the process of maturing in God, even though He is not finished with us, it is good. He is not finished and we are not yet perfected, but as long as we are maturing and enduring the process, it is good.

Hebrews 12:1-3 describes the process of growing in discipline as a race. "Therefore, we also, since we are surrounded by so great a cloud of witnesses, let us lay aside every weight, and the sin which so easily ensnares us, and let us run with endurance the race that is set before us, looking unto Jesus, the author and finisher of our faith, who for the joy that was set before Him endured the Cross, despising the shame, and has sat down at the right hand of the throne of God."

From the get-go, the writer of Hebrews tells us we are in a race. It is not a race for the swift, it is not a sprint and stop, but rather it is a race that those who enter run to win. Paul said in I Corinthians 9:24-27, "I am running to win and when I run to win it means I discipline myself and I do things that I normally would not do and I even do things that I do not have to do because they are expedient for me, because they are helping me with what I am doing." Paul is saying, whatever is not helping me with this race I am laying aside.

If you have ever tried to run for exercise or pleasure, you have seen other runners. They normally wear really little shorts, little shoes, and little shirts. Like you and me, when they started they wore big sweat pants and a big shirt to hide everything. Then, after they begin to get into shape, they replaced their larger clothing with something that was less wind resistant. Runners understand that larger clothing prevents them from running as efficiently as they could with less on. It is the same principle in our Christian walk. Anything that does not have to do with finishing well, we do not want to hang on to. We want to remove it so we can finish. Many begin the race but few finish. Our goal should be to not only finish, but to finish well.

I want to be like Paul, who at the end of the day was able to say, I have finished my course, I kept the faith, I have fought a good fight, now there is a reward for me. Finishing this race is about running well, looking to Jesus, the author and finisher of our faith because the good work that He started, He is going to finish. It encourages me to know He is going to finish what He started.

How do we finish? We have to embrace our cross just as Jesus did in Hebrews 12:2, "For the joy that was set before Jesus, He endured the Cross." Whatever the work of the Cross is doing in your life in the form of discipline there will be a reward when that part of the process has come to an end. On the other side of correction and discipline God has a specific assignment that we are designed to accomplish. Knowing Him intimately gives us a clear understanding that we are going to make it when we get through to the other side of whatever issue needs to be addressed and corrected and that we are going to be a whole lot better than when we started.

There is a price and a prize for discipline. It is not easy to be disciplined and to allow God to work in our lives. Believe me, I know. I have had a weight problem most of my life with the scales going up and down, but I made a decision to be disciplined in that area of my life. When I traveled a lot, we would eat late at night so I ran every day to stay in shape.

I did not always want to get up and do it, but I did because I was enjoying the benefits of health, strength, energy, and staying fit. However, for the past two or three years I have not done anything physical to keep in shape. I have played a few sports from time to time, but nothing really structured or disciplined. I knew I was getting a bit older and that I lacked discipline, so I said, "I am going to start running again."

I was pretty determined about it, so I jumped right out there on the road and ran. I used to be a pretty decent runner. Yet there I was running and I started feeling things I never even knew I had. I was running down the road and I knew I was not doing too well when a guy in a pickup truck rolled down his window and said, "Hey buddy, do you need some help?" Well, that certainly put it in perspective for me that if I was going to run to stay in shape I was going to have to make a true commitment to run faithfully and become disciplined to train. Of course, I hated every second of it in the beginning, but I began to experience results almost immediately and was reminded once again of the wonderful benefits from being disciplined, not only in exercise, but in every area of my life.

Persistence in running has strengthened me physically, and I really do feel fit and more alert. It was not fun in the beginning, but I knew I needed to get into shape. That caused me to become more disciplined, and now I am enjoying the benefits of staying the course and remaining disciplined in this pursuit. There has to be something that causes us to recognize we need discipline in areas of our lives.

Most of us will never succeed in disciplining ourselves for discipline's sake. I cannot tell you how many programs I have been on. I have tried many but have finished few. There has to be something that causes us to finish well that is greater than our desire to quit. For example, you can tell somebody to quit smoking for health purposes and they just cannot quit. Yet if they are told they have lung cancer, they will quit just like that. Try telling somebody to stop eating rich, fried foods, or starchy and sweet foods, and they respond with no, no, no. Tell these same people they have sugar diabetes and they immediately start a healthy, fat-free, sugar and starch free regime.

God's Plan and Purpose

There will always be reasons that make us try to become self-disciplined, but God does not want us to get to that place. He wants us to live by the Word of God and be led by His Holy Spirit. It is not because He wants to hurt us, He wants us to understand the principles He has set in place for us to live by and to be successful living them. God does not want us to die of lung cancer, sugar diabetes, or any other debilitating disease. God does not want us to fail in spiritual, physical, emotional, or financial areas of our life. So, we have to become disciplined in our understanding of God's plan and purpose for us. Many of us need to be disciplined in the area of our finances. Instead of following MasterCard's slogan to master the possibilities we need to *not* master the possibilities if our spending habits are putting us further and further into debt.

Emotional eating or buying is not God's plan either. I am an emotional person; I buy and eat out of emotion. I had to learn to recognize that if I allowed my emotions to rule my life, I would have a one hundred thousand dollar credit card bill, a big stomach, and a freezer full of ice cream. These may not seem to be significant training grounds, but if we listen to God's instructions and learn to live by His principles, we will realize He has small ways of training us for the big race if we will only pay attention.

The first way God disciplines our lives is found in Hebrews 12:3, "For consider Him who endured such hostility from sinners against Himself, lest you become weary and discouraged in your souls." We are still learning about enduring through discouraging times. This passage of Scripture is discussing persecution. God often allows persecution to become a disciplinary action in our lives. Persecution is not a possibility, it is a promise. In John 15: 19-21 Jesus said, "If they hated Me they're going to hate you." He also said, "If they talked about Me, they are going to talk about you." Jesus said, "If they persecuted and reviled Me, they are going to persecute and revile you; but rejoice when they do because great is your reward and the glory of God is going to rest on you."

I know that is not popular teaching, to promise persecution, but believe me, when we really sell out for God and want Him to work in our lives, He is going to use persecution for our benefit. If you are not experiencing any persecution right now, check on how brightly you are letting your light shine. Because if your light is shining brightly, it should attract a bit of persecution. Seriously, I am not talking about carrying a ten-pound Bible around with us everywhere we go. I read this recently and it seems appropriate here, "Share the gospel always and use words when necessary. It is living by example, for Jesus that is the topic." Honestly, letting your light shine in a very powerful way draws persecution. Jesus promised it was going to happen. It is proof that we are His disciples. John 15:20 tells us that the disciple will not be above the Master so it makes perfect sense that if He was persecuted *for His good works* we too will be tried, tested, and tempted when we attempt to accomplish the goal of spreading the Good News of the gospel.

So, when we are suffering persecution it may come from work, family, friends, or relatives. It just proves that we are disciples of Christ, and that Christ is working in us His disciplinary actions to bring strength, life, and liberty to our lives. It also proves that we are not of this world. John 15:18-19 tells us, "If you are of the world they would love you, but because you are not of the world, they are going to hate you. And they are going to persecute you. And they are going to say all manner of evil against you, but rejoice when they do because this is proof that we are not of this world. We are in it, but we are not of it we are born from above."

My favorite Scripture about persecution is in Mark 10:29 which states this, "No man has left houses, brethren, mother, sister, family, or anything for the kingdom of God's sake that he will not receive in this life an hundred fold return *with persecution*." Persecution is a sure sign that the hundred-fold blessing is about to come upon our lives.

Persecution comes with the promises of God. I will be honest with you, I do not like persecution. I like for everybody to like me, but not everyone does. I have suffered some persecution in my life as I have grown in the Kingdom of God, but the end result has always been one that has benefited my spiritual walk.

When I first became a follower of Christ I was known as the Jesus freak, a holy-roller and whatever, but remember when you first gave your life to the Lord and you wanted to tell everybody about it? I bet you took a few hits as well. We all deal with persecution from somewhere, and unfortunately it is usually from our families and friends that we thought would be thrilled for us. I am constantly amazed at the people that come to our churches who have to fight just to go to a service. Husbands persecute wives, wives persecute husbands, families persecute children who have answered the call to live for Jesus, teenagers in high schools are suffering persecution because they pray and attend church. The most shocking thing is how strongly people are persecuted, not by the world, *but by other churches,* because of where they worship or what they believe.

God is training a strong generation and persecution is part of the process. What is being learned by persevering persecution is making all of us stronger in our relationship with God and strengthening our conviction to serve Him regardless of how difficult the trials become. There are many kinds of persecution, but when we finally come to the point that we are being persecuted as Jesus was, we can *empathize*, not just *sympathize* with what Jesus experienced. He spoke clearly when He explained in John 15:20, "If they did it to Me, they will do it to you." Christians around the world have suffered many persecutions for believing in Jesus. It is when we realize that we have the same rewards as Jesus that we can finally rejoice in trials and tribulations.

I have learned that if we are not really accomplishing much for the Kingdom, we do not have to worry too much about suffering persecution. The other side of that coin is that if we really want God to work in our lives and see the benefits of discipline, we are going to suffer some form of persecution. My flesh does not like it one bit, but God *does* use persecution as discipline training.

God may be asking the hard questions, "Do you trust Me, or are you trusting culture and the world system? Are you going to endure and keep serving Me or are you going to allow persecution to defeat you?" Many of us suffer persecution for serving God, but the good news is if we will endure it there is a blessing on the other side.

According to I Corinthians 10:13, "There is no temptation taken you but such as is common to man: but God is faithful, who will not suffer you to be tempted above that you are able; but will with the temptation also make a way to escape, that you may be able to bear it." God always makes a way of escape, but it may not look like what we were hoping for. We have to remember that we are to learn from whatever experience we are in the middle of and that the only reason we are in it is because God wants to bring discipline to that area of our lives. God allows temptations and trials to come our way to discipline us in very specific areas of our lives. Trust me, God knows what area we need it in most.

God does not always give us what we want but He does always give us the tools we need to live in His will. We have to trust our Father that He is giving us something that will ultimately be for our good and His glory.

The Amplified version of I Corinthians 10:13 states, "For no temptation, no trial as enticing to sin, no matter how it comes or where it leads, has overtaken you and laid hold on you that is not common to man." That is, no temptation or trial is beyond human resistance. Every situation and circumstance has been applied, adjusted and adapted so that it belongs uniquely to the human experience. Jesus was tried on every side, by every torment and temptation, as a man, so we as mortal men can overcome.

God Is Faithful

God is faithful to His Word and has a compassionate nature. He can be trusted to not let us be tempted, tried, and assailed beyond our ability and strength of resistance and power to endure. With temptation, He will always provide a way out, a means of escape to a landing place. I like that, *a landing place*. That means we may be flying in turbulence right now, but God is going to bring us to a safe landing place and give us a way out. God has worked in my life through trials, temptations, and tribulation. He has always been faithful to never put me through more than I could bear.

I have come to look at it like this, the size of our temptation and trial is equal to the size of our value in the Kingdom of God. As controversial as that may seem, that is the way God does things. Because of our value, He will allow a trial to match the potential value of what He wants to do with us in the Kingdom of God. That is why many of us have been through severe trials. It is because we are very valuable to the Kingdom and God wants to produce genuine faith in us that is going to be used for His glory and His purposes. Many of us have been tested and tried by temptations, and many who are reading this are struggling right now. The good news is we are not going to live in trials forever.

Isaiah 43:2 encourages us with these words: You will go through the fire, but you will not be burned; you will go in the water, but you will not drown. You will be in the river, but it will not overflow and you will come out on the other side with more than you went in with. These promises are ours as we endure trials and tribulations and allow God to bring discipline to our lives. I am going to remind you once again, these times are not always joyous and it may take a while to get to the shouting and rejoicing part. However, in Hebrews 12:2 "Jesus, for the joy set before Him, endured the Cross." Whatever the Cross is working in our lives right now, if we will endure it, when we come out on the other side, we will be stronger than when we went in and we will understand more of the plans and purposes of God.

Truthfully, I have never grown closer to God in times of success, only in times of trial. Jesus said in Matthew 12:27, "What I tell you in darkness; that, speak in the light." God does not speak a lot in the light of the good times, He always speaks in darkness. The good news is that when we are in darkness, the darkest is just before the new dawn. When we are in dark times, God is working discipline in our lives. As we endure, midnight will turn to dawn, the new day is going to rise, and we are going to come out with more than we went in with because we endured.

The truth is that right now, in our society and culture, God is on trial in many lives and He is going to prove whether He is faithful or not. Like Sarah in Hebrews 11:11 we will judge God and find Him faithful. It is crucial that we understand that trials are not just for trial's sake. They are specifically designed to correct areas in our lives and to prove that God is Who He says that He is and will accomplish what He has said He will accomplish. God is able to make a way of escape, and two things are for sure: God can be trusted and will never allow us to be tempted above what we are able to bear. With every trial God is going to give us a way out. He is always right in the middle of the fire with us.

Right in the midst of the fire of trials is where we are the closest to God. He has to be close enough to keep His hand on our pulse to see when too much is too much. In Daniel 3:25 when the Hebrew children, Meshack, Shadrack, and Abindgo, were in the fire, there was another Man with them, the fourth Man, Who looked like the Son of God. In the fire the only thing that burned were the ropes that were holding them. God is not out to destroy us. He is faithful to discipline us, and the only things He wants to destroy are whatever is preventing us from running this race and finishing well. The only thing that is going to burn is what is not of Him.

We may still go to church yet feel isolated when we are in the heat of a fiery trial. Everybody else seems happy while we are baking in a hot oven. It seems as though Jesus comes by, looks in at us, and we think, "Oh God, we are about to get out of this." Then He opens the oven door and surprise, we haven't finished baking yet. The good news is that in trials and temptations what God wants to burn is the chaff in our lives, not us.

If we will allow God to discipline us in every area of our lives, through trials and temptations, our tests will be turned into testimonies. Our trials will be turned into triumphs and our messes will be turned into messages. The only thing God wants to do is make us more effective. When we come out on the other side of adversity, just like in 2 Corinthians 1:4, we will be able to comfort others with the same comfort we have been comforted with. Plus, we will be able to testify to others and tell them, "Hang on, God is faithful. He brought me out and He will bring you out too." That is what God wants to produce in us.

Luke 22:32 tells the story of when Jesus said to Peter, "Satan has desired to sift you." What is sifting? Sifting is when wheat is put in a box with little rocks and shaken together to get rid of the chaff to get to the pure wheat. The rocks and chaff stay in the basket, and the wheat falls down to be collected and made into flour. God puts us in that sifting basket and as we endure sifting, He makes us faithful. There is an old saying that you cannot make an able man faithful, but God sure can make a faithful man able.

Personally, that has to be what I love most about serving God. All the junk (and God knows just how much junk I really have had to be relieved of) has to stay behind and only the good makes it through. We all want the bad stuff to be in the past with only the good things of God manifesting in the present and our future. It is when that happens that we are going to become very productive for God. Jesus said it like this to Peter in Luke 22:31, "Satan has desired to sift you, but I have prayed for you that your faith is not going to fail." It is so encouraging to me when somebody comes and says, "Kent, I am praying for you." That encourages me, but how about this? Jesus said, "I am praying for you." He said, "I have prayed for you and your faith is not going to fail."

When we do not have an ounce of faith left, we can stand on the promise that Jesus has already prayed for us and our faith is not going to fail. The junk is going to be consumed in the fire and what is good will remain. We will come out of whatever trial, tribulation, or travail with victory, power, and an even greater glory is going to abide within because the trying of our faith is more precious than the trying of gold. At the end of the day the victory over these very issues is going to produce genuine people with genuine faith. That is why God has allowed us to go through the fire, because He wants us to be genuine.

I do not want to live with people who have not been through the fire. Those who have been through the refining fire are genuine. When they tell you they are praying, you can write it down, they are praying. They are not judging us by what we are going through, because they have been through so much themselves. There are times we have all felt as though we have had the hell beaten out of us. *That* is God's doing. He is getting all the chaff out and allowing the gold on the inside of us to shine through us to reach this lost and dying world.

Do Not Despise the Disciplining of the Lord

Hebrews 12:6 tells us, "My son, do not despise the disciplining of the Lord, nor be discouraged when you are rebuked by Him; for whom the Lord loves He disciplines, and scourges every son whom He receives." When we endure discipline, God deals with us as sons—persecution, trials, tribulation, and correction are the tools He uses. *Now,* I handle persecution pretty well and have even learned to endure during trials and tribulations. However, I still do not like to be corrected. I do not mind if God corrects me; the only problem is that God often uses people to do it. The lesson for us is that we serve an invisible God and that the Body of Christ often gets to deliver His message to mankind. The point being we have to learn to receive correction through other people.

It would be different if Jesus always talked to me about areas that I need to improve in directly but He lets my wife tell me certain things and she is always right. I hate that, especially when I am driving. Before we had GPS capability, I WOULD NOT stop and ask directions. My wife calls me Christopher Columbus because I always find our destinations by accident. She is patient at first, and then she always says, "Honey, you need to stop and ask where we are because we are not on the right road." I always respond by saying, "Yes, we are. Who is driving this car?" She answers, "You are and that is what I am afraid of."

One time we were following a man home to eat dinner with him. We were driving behind him discussing our counsel for him because he had been going through some financial problems, and we were going to pray with him. My wife and I were talking as I was driving. My wife asked, "Are you sure we are going the right way?" And I said, "Sure, we are following the guy." She said, "OK, but are you sure?" I said, "Yeah, yeah, we are following him."

We continued to follow the car ahead of us and as we arrived I said, "Well, no wonder he is in financial trouble, he is living way above his means." We had pulled into the driveway of a huge home that was beautifully landscaped. A man got out of the car in front of us and it *was not* who I was supposed to be following. Somehow I had gotten behind the wrong car.

The man asked, "Why have you been following me?" I said, "We are supposed to meet someone here." But he was not the man we were supposed to pray with, and you talk about being embarrassed. My wife suspected I was following the wrong car all along, and as soon as she realized it she began to ask the questions that could have corrected the situation if only I had listened. All I had to do was stop being prideful, call and make sure we were following the right man.

Another prideful moment that I am not particularly proud of happened a few years ago while we were taping television programs in our studio. By that time I had been doing television work for years and felt like I knew a little bit about it. I do not know a lot, but I do know a little. Anyway, at this taping we had done about sixteen programs and we were finishing up the last one. The very last one I did something that is bad to do in television. If a camera gets real close to you, even if you weigh one hundred and fifty pounds, a wrong angle can make you look as if you weigh three hundred and fifty pounds. If the camera gets right up on your face, your head will look like a camel's head.

There are certain cameras you are supposed to look into to make it a professional shot. Right at the end I did not do the right thing, and the camera caught a shot that was pretty funny looking. Anyway, I knew I had done the wrong thing and as soon as we got through my wife said, "That was a bad angle for you, let's reshoot that last segment." Of course, I said, "No, its fine." However, I knew it wasn't fine. She responded, "No, sweetheart, let's just reshoot it." I said, "No, I did it right. Let's look at it." We had our producer rerun it and I said, "Oh yeah, it looks fine." I knew it did not look fine. My response was, "Bev, you are not supposed to be here this morning." Wrong answer! If I had admitted I was wrong and received correction that exchange could have ended quickly. After a *mild*, prolonged discussion, and an apology (mine to her), we went back and we did it right.

The thing is it is often difficult to receive correction because we take it personally. Because we take it personally as opposed to instructionally, we perceive we are being rejected. Perhaps we become insecure because we did not do the right thing, but correction gives us the opportunity to make things right even if we do not like the message, the messenger, or the meaning. However, when we allow correction to do its work in us, it will produce a good work in us. Unfortunately, the reason most of us cannot receive correction is because people have not given it to us correctly and it comes across as judgmental as opposed to instructive.

There is a right and wrong way to bring correction to someone's life. If correction is presented in love, I do not mind anybody correcting me. However, if you do not love me, and you are just trying to push your agenda, do not try to correct me. When people write me letters of correction and do not sign them, I wad them up and throw them in the trash. I do not receive correction from anyone who does not love me enough to let me know who they are. God wants us to correct one another, yet He wants us to extend and receive correction from those who love us and who really want to see effectual change in our lives. He operates through anyone who approaches us in godly love to see our lives changed, and when we allow God to discipline us and bring correction to our lives, powerful things begin to happen.

One of the most powerful things that occurs is that our minds are illuminated and we do not remain ignorant of God's power, plans, purposes, and provision. We learn from Proverbs 12:1 that, "Whoever loves instruction, loves knowledge, but he who hates correction is stupid." Proverbs 1:22 continues that thought, "How long you simple ones will you love simplicity. For scorners delight in their scorning, but fools hate knowledge." Proverbs 15:31 goes further, "The ear that hears the rebukes of life will abide among the wise, it will keep you prosperous." Proverbs 13:18 makes it even clearer, "Poverty and shame will come to him who disdains correction, but he who regards a rebuke will be honored." Proverbs 15:10 is downright direct, "Harsh discipline is for him who forsakes the way and he who hates correction will die."

Discipline will keep us alive and on a straight and narrow path and keep us in God's will. Proverbs 10:17 directs us, "He who keeps instruction is in the way of life, but he who refuses correction goes astray." Proverbs 27:5 sums it all up, "Open rebuke is better than concealed love." When we really love somebody, we must tell them the truth, in love. If they know we really love them, they should receive correction from us.

From Hero to Zero

I am learning to receive correction and I am endeavoring to become better at that in my life. I believe if we were all honest, we are all trying to get better at it. Nobody really likes correction because it is personal. I love when people come up to me after a conference or a church service and say, "Man that was a great message." On the inside I am "the man", but on the outside I behave properly and give Him the praise. Everybody likes to be encouraged and I am no different.

Then the corrections and the rebukes happen and I go from hero to zero. That is when discouragement tries to defeat me. Believe me, I have been corrected and *discouraged*, and I have been corrected and *encouraged*. I have ministered and people have come up to me and said, "Kent, you said this and you said that and I do not believe that is quite accurate." When they do it in love, and I know they love me, I can gladly say, "Wow, you may be right. I am going to research that and if proves to be right then great, I will make the correction." I am able to receive that and grow from the experience. The flip side of that is when somebody comes to me and behaves in a haughty, arrogant manner with pointing fingers, condemning me, that potential correction becomes an accusation and is really difficult to receive.

We need to learn how to give and receive correction in godly love. As we do, we will continue to mature in our spiritual gifts. As our character develops each of our individual gifts will be more effective as we endeavor to further the Kingdom. As we learn, we are going to walk in the power of God's love and demonstrate it to others. As we continue to endure and embrace correction we will handle persecution, discipline, trials and temptations with greater grace and a better understanding.

Remember, there is always a prize on the other side of correction. Many times when we are being disciplined, whether it be through trials, persecutions, or correction, it does not *feel* good. No trial seems joyous for the present, but painful. However, in the end, it is for our own profit and according to Hebrews 12:11 will yield the peaceable fruit of righteousness. Often, when we are in the middle of whatever learning experience God has designed for us, it may seem as though He has left us hanging and there is no end in sight. Recently, I felt that way. I could not really put my finger on any particular trial I was going through, but I did realize it was a time of disciplining in which God was doing something in my life.

I went into my office, sat down and asked, "God, I feel I have lost the anointing and Your Presence. Have I done something? Have I offended somebody? Have I said the wrong thing?" I began to search my life and my heart. Right in the middle of this tirade I sensed God's Presence, and He said, "I forsook the Anointed One, so you would be one anointed and so I would never forsake you." Those words shook me to my very core. I believe God was saying to me, "No matter what you are going through and what you are feeling, you are anointed. It is not because of anything you do. The only reason you are anointed is because I forsook the Anointed One and the reason I will never forsake you is because I forsook Him."

Correction and discipline has nothing to do with the way we feel. God spoke these words to me, "Just endure." I asked, "What do

You mean, Lord? He said, "My power is released in continuing." I was reminded of Galatians 6:9, "Continue in well doing and you will reap if you faint not." Then in Colossians 4:2, "Continue in prayer." Next was John 8:31, "Continue in the Word." These were followed by Acts 13:43, "Continue in the grace of God." And next came Hebrews 13:1, "Continue is brotherly love," and Ephesians 5:18, "Continually be filled with the Spirit." Finally He ended with Psalm 34:1, "Praise shall continually come out of your mouth."

God encouraged me by saying, "If you will continue doing the right things, keep praising and honoring Me, keep being fed by My Word, keep praying, keep letting love flow through you, then My power is going to be released in whatever situation you are in." When we endure, we are going to come out on the other side and we are going to have more of God's plans, promises and provision than we went in with. We are going to learn to enjoy the discipline of God because we are going to know for sure that He is treating us as sons.

Sometimes God, as our Daddy, has to discipline our lives. It is life-changing when we understand why He is doing it. The reason is profound in its implications. He disciplines us because we are valuable to Him. If we were not valuable to God, there would be no need for us to be chastened or disciplined. The only reason we go through training is because there is something on the inside of us that is valuable to Him. He has to get rid of the old to establish the new. That is why Paul encourages us in Hebrews 12:1 to lay aside everything that is going to keep us from running this race and continuing. When we lay everything down we begin to recognize that the discipline of God is producing in us more effectiveness, grace and love. God is proving to us like never before that He really is our Father. When we endure discipline as a son and do not despise His correction, there is joy on the other side of the Cross. Hebrews 12:2 reminds us that for the joy set before Him, He endured the Cross and Psalm 30:5 encourages us that weeping may endure for the night, but joy comes in the morning.

To live a life of good success, God wants us to embrace discipline and learn how to endure so He can bring us out on the other side of testing more mature than when we went in. When we are in a time of being disciplined, there is only one thing happening. God is increasing and we are decreasing. As He increases, we automatically decrease. All we have to do is endure. As we continue to endure, He will increase in our lives and the things that are not pleasing to Him will decrease. God will remove anything that is preventing us from running this race and finishing well.

Wisdom

Wisdom: Ability to discern inner qualities and relationships.
"Behind my pride there lives a me that knows humility."- India Aire

Chapter Eight

Prayerfully, as we have read this text, God has kept us moving on our journey to "good success." We have learned about obedience, favor, trusting the Lord, the fear of the Lord, honoring the Lord with our possessions, the correction of the Lord, and now we will learn where wisdom fits into the process. Interestingly, the first twelve verses in Proverbs Chapter Three are about living a practical application of all of these subjects. The next twelve verses speak primarily about wisdom.

Verses 13-26 unfolds God's plan for those who walk in wisdom. "Happy is the man who finds wisdom, and the man who gains understanding; for her proceeds are better than the profits of silver and her gain than fine gold. She is more precious than rubies and all the things you may desire cannot be compared to her. Length of days is in her right hand and in her left hand art riches and honor and her ways are the ways of pleasantness. All her paths are peace. She is a tree of life to those who take hold of her and happy are all those who retain her. The Lord, by wisdom, founded the earth and by understanding established the heavens. By His knowledge the depths were broken up and clouds dropped down the dew. My son, let them not depart from your eyes. Keep sound wisdom and discretion, so they will be life to your soul and grace to your neck. Then you will walk safely in your way and your foot will not stumble. When you lie down, you will not be afraid. Yes, you will lie down and your sleep will be sweet. Do not be afraid of sudden terror nor the trouble from the wicked one that comes. For the Lord will be your confidence and will keep your foot from being caught." The results of walking in wisdom are some of the most powerful promises in the whole of Scripture.

Proverbs 4:5-7 states, "Get wisdom, get understanding. Do not forget nor turn away from the words of My mouth. Do not forsake her and she will preserve you. Love her and she will keep you. Wisdom is the principle thing, therefore, get wisdom and in all your getting, get understanding."

God is telling us very plainly that our main focus should not be wealth, knowledge, education, or anything that is not built on the foundation of God's wisdom. His Word admonishes us to obtain and apply godly wisdom to every area of our lives before we ever make a decision about anything else.

Once we seek wisdom, God's provision and power will be given to us. God calls wisdom, Her. The Greek word for wisdom is *Sophia*. Common wisdom is: common sense, prudence, skill, and a right application of knowledge. We have all met people that we know who are brilliant. However, they do not seem to be able to cope with the everyday minutiae of life, or to make the simplest of common sense decisions.

Common sense is not really common sense at all. Common sense is really uncommon sense because people who have good reasoning skills do not gain them from earthly or natural means. That kind of wisdom comes from the Spirit of Wisdom Who is the Holy Spirit of God. Wisdom comes from God and common sense is uncommon sense. This understanding is the kind of wisdom that God wants us to have and to live experientially. Wisdom is valuable and comes from God. Every area of our lives is enriched when we seek godly wisdom first. Wisdom makes us rich spiritually, naturally, and emotionally.

The Proceeds of Wisdom

In Proverbs 3:14 the proceeds of wisdom are better than the profits of silver and her gain is better than fine gold. She is more precious than rubies and all the things we desire cannot be compared to her. Length of days is in her right hand and in her left hand are riches and honor. Her ways are ways of pleasantness and all her paths are peace. She is a tree of life to those who take hold of her and happy are all those that retain her.

God approached Solomon in I Kings 3:9-11 just after Solomon's coronation as king and asked, "What do you want? Anything you want you may have." Solomon thought about his answer and he chose the correct response. He said, "Give me wisdom." In the times we live, not many of us would have answered that way. Our responses would probably be a more natural response to have our immediate needs met: God pay off my American Express, let me drop ten pounds, do this, and do that. There are many things we want and earnestly believe we need. However, Solomon knew something about God. He said, "God give me Your wisdom," and God responded, "Because you have asked the best thing, I am going to give you riches, honor, and a good, long life with peace and prosperity."

Once we seek, and find the wisdom of God, we have found good success. Interestingly enough, Scripture tells us to live a blessed life we must *find* it. That means we are to search and research wisdom. It is not something that falls into our laps. Wisdom is something we go after and when found, we embrace.

The Tree of Life

Wisdom is known in the Bible as a Tree of Life. The wisdom of God versus the wisdom of the world is an age-old battle that wages in our minds. In Genesis 3:6, when the enemy of our souls tempted Eve to eat of the Tree of Knowledge of Good and Evil, he tempted her by appealing to her pride. He said, "If you eat this, you are going to be wise just like God and you are going to know everything God knows."

The same thing that caused Satan to fall caused Eve to eat the forbidden fruit. Pride destroyed Adam and Eve's destiny by introducing the world system and *carnal* knowledge into Paradise where the wisdom of God reigned until that devastating choice was made. In an instant, their world as they had known it was destroyed. Colossians 2: 17-19 tells us that the knowledge of the world puffs us up whereas the wisdom of God builds us up.

I have many friends who were afforded a college education. They left for college full of common sense and came back with not much common sense at all. These young men and women left home fearing God, strong in their faith, and came back almost agnostic because they were puffed up with knowledge and philosophy. Unfortunately, it is not only the secular realm that this anomaly occurs because the same thing happens in Bible colleges. Knowledge without godly wisdom puffs us up and destroys the intimacy that God designed us to live in with Him.

God is the same yesterday, today, and forever and we still have a choice that we have to make in the contemporary times in which we live. It is the same choice Eve made in the Garden. We have to choose the knowledge of the world or the wisdom of God. When we choose the knowledge of the world, innocence is lost just as it was from the moment Eve's eyes were opened to her nakedness. She immediately lost the childlike faith that creates the atmosphere to live in God's wisdom, while developing His character without worldly influences.

There are many directives in the Bible that we may not ever understand, but it isn't too much of a stretch to understand that God had His reasons for Adam and Eve not tasting this particular fruit, that is, the fruit of carnal knowledge. Not eating from the Tree of the Knowledge of Good and Evil was the only limitation God placed on them in their relationship with Him. They literally had freedom to eat from any other tree, make plans, build, think, reason, and experience all of the ordinary things we all do. God's protection for them was their innocence from the knowledge of sin.

His desire was that their trust in Him would be so established they would never have to go beyond the protection He had covered them with. He did not explain all of that to Adam and Eve. In fact, He knew they were going to sin against His wisdom even before they did. So, if that is in fact correct, theologically and historically, what was the point? Theoretically the answer is simple. Children trust their parents to make right choices for them and they obey because they trust them.

That is exactly what God was hoping for from our ancestral parents. He wanted them to choose wisdom because they trusted that He knew best. Trust is the beginning of the fear of the Lord and the beginning of wisdom. He wanted His children to trust that He, as their Creator and heavenly Father, knew what was best for them. Psalm 111:10 assures us that, "The fear of the Lord is the beginning of wisdom; a good understanding have all those who do His commandments. His praise endures forever. The beginning of wisdom is the fear of the Lord."

He wanted them to *choose* to obey His instruction because He said so, just like we do, as children, when we are obedient to our parents. God said, "Do not eat of this tree. The other ones you can have, but do not eat of this one." They should have obeyed because He said so. We have to learn to recognize the enemy tries to steal the reverential fear of the Lord by tempting us to walk in our own counsel not ever seeking God's plan for our lives. The reality is that all the while God is encouraging us to make the right choices through His Word and His promises. It is when we stop obeying His established principles and walking in His wisdom that we, like Adam and Eve, lose our innocence.

We have to understand that we can mature and still be innocent. Actually, most people with godly wisdom are innocent. What does that mean? They believe there is something good in everybody. They are not judgmental. They are innocent in their faith and in their beliefs, and they are not complicated. Most wise people are not complicated. They answer questions in a simple, wise manner. It is easy to be entreated, gentle, kind and walk in meekness when we live in the fear of the Lord, full of His wisdom. The knowledge of the world is prideful and arrogant, so it stands to reason God's wisdom would be the opposite of that. The knowledge of God is meek, gentle, and kind.

Still, we have a choice to make. Over twenty years ago, I walked away from God and the atmosphere of innocence that I was raised in. I have told many people that I came to the Lord through a drug problem.

My mama and daddy *drug* me to church every time the doors were open. Many of us grew up in a spiritual atmosphere and had to go church. When my parents were asked, "Why do I have to go?" The answer was always consistent, "because I said so." I sat through boring sermons and all sorts of church stuff that meant absolutely nothing to me at the time. I got so many spankings in church because I was always acting up. However, there was an atmosphere of innocence there that even though I did not understand it at the time, godly seeds were being sown into my destiny even as I threw spitballs and misbehaved.

I never heard ugly, four letter words, or vulgar things and was never exposed to that kind of environment. There was a real spirit of innocence in the home that I was raised in. Yet there came a day of reckoning for me when I made the choice to live outside of the covering and protection that I had always known in a godly home. I could have stayed on that path and chosen the Tree of Life, but I chose the Tree of the Knowledge of Good and Evil.

I stood in a shower in the house I was raised in and told God this, "God, if You will give me the next few years to go enjoy the world and find out what it has to offer, I will come back and serve You later. " That was the day I chose the wrong tree. Moreover, I got out there and found that there is definitely more evil than good in the world that I had chosen.

Innocence Lost

I had been raised in an atmosphere of innocence, so when I got out in the world and heard vulgar things, the words pierced me. *At first,* I reacted to each curse word, but before I knew it, I grew immune to them and started speaking that way and thought nothing about it. I lost my innocence. That is why God says if we want to be in the Kingdom, we have to be born again and become a child with childlike faith and innocence. That is the wisdom of God.

Kindness, meekness, and gentleness is the wisdom of God. Because of the Cross of Christ, we now have the ability to choose right or wrong. The Cross not only bought back our lives but also bought back our ability to make a choice. However, we still have to choose. Under sin and slavery, we did not have the right to choose, but now, because of the Cross, we have the right to choose. God is pro-choice. He will not override what we choose. We are back in the Garden of Eden because of the power made available to us, by the Cross, to choose. We can choose life, blessing, health, and strength or we can choose the Tree of the Knowledge of Good and Evil, death, and all that death holds.

The world system dictates that we earn wisdom. Worldly wisdom tells us we have to be a certain caliber of person. The world has many ways of saying salvation can be earned. Some of the hardest people to win to Christ are those who are upstanding, moral citizens, who think that they have no sin issues because they are good people. They do not chew or hang around with those who do. They keep the rules and they *are* good citizens. Yet they still have to make the choice to eat of the Tree of Life and wisdom, or not. To the world this saying is foolishness, but to God and to us who are saved, it is wisdom. I Corinthians 1:18, 21-30 tells us something very powerful. "I know very well how foolish the message of the Cross sounds to those who are on the road to destruction, but we who are saved recognize this message as the very power of God. For since, in the wisdom of God, the world through wisdom did not know God, it pleased God through the foolishness of the message preached to save those who believe. For Jews request a sign, and Greeks seek after wisdom; but we preach Christ crucified, to the Jews a stumbling block and to the Greeks foolishness, but to those who are called, both Jews and Greeks, Christ the power of God and the wisdom of God. Because the foolishness of God is wiser than men, and the weakness of God is stronger than men. For you see your calling, brethren, that not many wise according to the flesh, not many mighty, not many noble, *are called.* But God has chosen the foolish things of the world to put to shame the wise, and God has chosen the weak things of the world to put to shame the things which are mighty; and the base things of the world and the things which are despised God has chosen, and the things which are not, to bring to nothing the things that are that no flesh should glory in His presence. But of Him you are in Christ Jesus, who became for us wisdom from God, and righteousness and sanctification and redemption."

God, in His wisdom, saw to it that the world would never find Him through human wisdom; He has used our foolish preaching to save *all* who believe. God's way seems foolish to the Jews because they want a sign from heaven to prove it is true. It is foolishness to the Greeks because they believe only what agrees with their own wisdom. When we preach Christ crucified, the Jews are offended and the Gentiles say it is nonsense. To those who are called by God, to salvation, Jews *and* Gentiles, Christ is the mighty power of God and the wonderful wisdom of God.

This foolish plan of God is far wiser than the wisest of human plans, and God's weakness is far stronger than the greatest of human strength. Few of us were wise, powerful, or wealthy in the world's eyes when God called us. Instead, God deliberately chose those things in the world that He considers foolish in order to shame those things that are wise. He chose those things that are powerless to shame those things that are powerful.

God chose people despised by the world, who were counted as nothing at all, and used them to bring something that the world considers important. No one can ever boast of what *they* have accomplished in the Presence of God. He and He alone, made it possible for us to be in Christ. For our benefit, God made Christ to be Wisdom. Wisdom is not a thing, He is a Person and His name is Jesus.

Janie Tinklenberg was on to something when she created the *What Would Jesus Do?* bracelet. If we want to know the wisdom of God, we should do what Jesus did, and would do. To find out what Jesus did, read the red. Every time He acted it was the wisdom of God being manifested.

The wisdom of God spoke through Jesus and confounded the Pharisees. Preachers and teachers can attest to moments when the wisdom of God literally begins to speak through them and lives are immediately impacted. That is the Spirit of the Wisdom of God being manifested in the earth today.

The church should be so full of wisdom that we cannot resist the Spirit of Wisdom wherever it is manifested and through whatever vessel God decides to use. In Acts 16:10 Stephen was an usher in the early church, and when he spoke it was with such godly wisdom that the people of his day could not resist what he had to say.

Recently, I went to the county jail. There was a young man there who was twenty years old and addicted to drugs. He was the father of an eight week old baby boy. He was in prison for using and distributing crystal methamphetamine. I was praying for the wisdom of God and asking, "What am I going to tell this guy?" I am not a counselor; I am not a trained psychologist. The Lord said, "Be quiet." I thought, "Well, that is the wisdom of God."

Proverbs 17:8 encourages us to remember that even a fool, when he does not say anything, is considered to be wise. Anytime we are in a situation and hear, "Be quiet," that is God. So I thought, well, I will just listen to what this young man has to say.

I did not plan on saying a thing when all of a sudden these words jumped out of me, "God did not send me here to preach to you. God sent me here to deliver you." I looked at that young man and his eyes opened wide. He and I both knew God was present and ready to move on his behalf.

His eyes were as big as saucers. I was on one phone and he was on the other with a glass partition between us. I asked "Do you want to be free?" He said, "Yes, I do." I said, "Pray this prayer with me." He prayed the sinner's prayer and with tears running down his face, he asked Jesus Christ, the Prince of Peace, the Mighty Savior, and the King of all wisdom, to come into his life. I saw a tangible demonstration of the wisdom, and power of God, transform him from the kingdom of darkness into the kingdom of light.

He said, "My God, I have never felt anything like that before." I looked across at that young man and said, "That is the Holy Spirit." I told him how God saved me and he said, "Man, I feel like chains were broken off of me."

He needed the power of God released in his life and deliverance manifested that day. I Corinthians 1:27 is very specific that God uses the foolish things of the world to confound the wise. Personally, I would rather be a fool for God than wise for the world. That is the kind of wisdom we need, always mindful that He who wins souls is wise. The wisdom of God is not just about living on earth in this realm; it is also about living eternally. That is the true wisdom of God. When we really have a revelation of the purpose of seeking the wisdom of God, we start doing what Jesus would do. We start acting like Jesus.

Jesus said, "Father, forgive them, they do not know what they are doing." He also told us to, "Turn the other cheek." That is the wisdom of God. Jesus said, "Bless them that persecute you. If you want to be great, become the least and become servant of all." How about this one? "Neither do I condemn you. Go and sin no more." What is that? That is the wisdom of God. Jesus is the manifested, manifold wisdom of God. When we choose Him, we are choosing wisdom itself.

Proverbs 8:23 relates that Wisdom was with God before the foundations of the earth and was with God when He said, "Let there be light," before the foundation of the earth was ever laid. Who was He talking about? He was talking about His Son. Jesus is the Wisdom of God. All we have to do to start walking in godly wisdom is choose Him.

The Five Senses

When we choose Him, we receive wisdom from God. James 3:13-15 answers the question, "How do we discern what is the wisdom of God, Who is wise and understanding among you? Let him show by good conduct that his works are done in the meekness of wisdom. But if you have bitter envy and self-seeking in your hearts, do not boast and lie against the truth. This wisdom does not descend from above, but is earthly, sensual, and demonic."

What does sensual mean? It means belonging to the natural or physical, unspiritual. It is living in the domain of the five senses. That is where most of us live. Most of us never enjoy the wisdom of God because we spend all of our lives living by our five senses. We live by what we can see, smell, taste, hear, and touch. God wants us to live in the spiritual realm with the Wisdom of God manifesting wisdom in every area of our lives, in business and at home.

How do we know the difference? Where envy and self-seeking exist, confusion is there and every evil work. God is not the author of confusion; He is the author of peace. If there is confusion when we are about to make a decision, we should stop and seek God's clear direction. When we experience peace, we know we are in the will of God. When we do not have peace, we should stop. How do we discern the wisdom of God? James 3:17 instructs us, "But the wisdom that is from above is first pure, then peaceable, gentle, willing to yield, full of mercy and good fruits, without partiality and without hypocrisy." When our lives are built on God's wisdom, we have everything that He has.

Pure love is demonstrated by those who have been through trials themselves. There is no agenda as mercy, love, and the grace of God is demonstrated because that is what has been shown to them. The wisdom of God is always pure without anything being mixed with it. When we seek the wisdom of God, peace and gentleness is right there with it. Gentleness means we are quick to listen to others and slow to speak about our own opinions and ambitions.

It is easy to rely on human reasoning and our five senses, but is not scriptural. When we started to build Word Alive International Outreach, if we had done things in the natural, according to our five senses, we would have never gotten off of the ground. I wanted to start in somebody's basement, with two or three people, then move to a shopping center, then perhaps get a tent, and work my way into the thing. That was my plan, but it was not God's. God wanted us to build a building and begin to have church. That was scary to me but it was the wisdom of God. God said, "Build it and they will come." We built and they came.

We were up and running for six months when God said, "Close services the month of July." That is definitely not human wisdom. Trust me, in the natural realm a church does not get started and six months later stop having services. God told us to take the month of July and give everybody a Sabbath month. We thought it was the boldest thing we had ever heard, but we gave it a try and God spoke to us through prophecy. He said, "What you are doing is like Elijah pouring water on the sacrifice. The only way the fire will burn and the only way that it will live is if I am doing it, not you." And He said, "I will prove I am building My church." That was the wisdom of God speaking to our spirit, not our five senses.

The Mercy of God

Wisdom is full of mercy. My wife and I have made a decision in our personal and ministerial lives that if we are going to err we are going to err on the side of mercy. If we are going to be persecuted for anything, it will be because we are too merciful. I truly do not believe we can be too merciful by giving people a second, a third, fourth, fifth, and a sixth, seventy times seven chances to get it right. We have to be merciful people because everyone needs mercy.

We may not know how to admit it, but at some point we all need the mercies of God. We all have weaknesses. Every weakness represented in humanity is represented in churches around the world each week. We may not know what weakness the person who is sitting next to us battles but be assured they have one. The wisdom of God will cause us to be merciful without partiality. What does that mean? In my opinion any church that is only one race is not built on the wisdom of God. There is no room for partiality, racism, or judgment in the house of God. There is no rich or poor, no Jew, nor Greek, Asian, white, nor black, nor Hispanic. We are all one new man in Christ Jesus without partiality and without hypocrisy.

The question is, "How do we get wisdom?" James 1:5 tells us to ask for it, "Does any man lack wisdom? Ask and God will give liberally to those that ask." I do not pray as much as I should each day, but there is one prayer that I get out of my mouth at some point every day and that is, "God give me wisdom. Give me wisdom because I realize that James 1:5 has promised me if I will ask for it, You will give it to me." The Word of God is where we find wisdom. II Timothy 3:15 reads, "The Scriptures are able to make you wise unto salvation." Psalm 119: 98-100 states, "By keeping Your precepts, (Your Word) I have become wiser than the aged men and wiser than even my teachers." So, how do we get the wisdom of God? We ask for it. Where do we get the wisdom of God? We receive wisdom by studying the Word of God. We are like computers and we download the Word before we can act on it. If we want the wisdom of God, we have to continually feed ourselves with the Word.

Some days I read the Bible and it does not make any sense to me at all, especially when I get over into Leviticus and Chronicles and somebody is begetting somebody and on it goes. I have been known to skip that part and go to the good part. I have come to realize that I really do get out of it what I have put into it, whether it is a long or short study time. Wisdom may not come all at once, but if we continue in well doing and do not grow weary the Word will be hidden in our hearts. Then, when a situation arises in which we need wisdom, a Scripture we may not even remember on our own will come right out of our spirit.

That is why David said, "I hid Your Word in my heart, that I would not sin against You." When we are about to make a wrong decision, a Scripture will come to mind and we will have the right Scripture for the right time. The Word of God brings wisdom through the Holy Spirit.

I Corinthians 2:11-12 tells us this, "Eye has not seen, ear has not heard, the mind cannot comprehend what God has for us, but it is revealed to us by the Spirit. The spirit of man knows the man, how much more the Spirit of God knows God, and will show us the things freely given to us by God." Once again, we do have to make the choice to seek wisdom and it is a daily choice. Every day that I wake up, I have a choice. In Deuteronomy 30:15 and 19, God said," I set before you life and death, blessing and cursing. Choose life."

The Cross bought back my choice, and *now*, I have to make one. I am free to choose *now*. I was not free to choose before. I can stand every day and make the right choice to follow God and to seek wisdom. Am I going to seek wisdom and the Tree of Life or I am going to seek knowledge and go the route of the Tree of the Knowledge of Good and Evil? Either I will follow pride, arrogance, my own way, prideful thoughts, and lust or I am going to follow the wisdom of God. God, in His infinite wisdom said, "Follow the Tree of Life and choose life."

Proverbs 9:1-6 tells us something very powerful, "Wisdom has built her spacious house with seven pillars. She has prepared a great banquet, mixed the wine, set the table. She has sent her servants to invite everyone to come. She calls out from the heights overlooking the city, saying come home with me. She urges the simple. To those without good judgment, she says come eat my food; drink the wine I've mixed. Leave your foolish ways behind and begin to live. Learn how to be wise."

Proverbs 9:13-18 tells us of the opposite of wisdom and that is worldly folly, "There is another woman calling and her name is folly. She is loud and brash. She is ignorant and does not even know it. She sits in her doorway on the heights overlooking the city and calls out to men and women going by who are minding their own business. Come home with me she urges the simple. To those without good judgment she says, stolen water is refreshing. Food eaten in secret tastes the best, but the men do not realize that her former guests are now in the grave of hell."

The Beginning of Wisdom and Knowledge

Every day we have two voices calling out to us. The wisdom of God, is calling, "Hey foolish ones, simple ones, turn in here." Then there is the wisdom of the world saying, "Do not forsake folly, come on over here with me. Pleasant bread is sweet. Pleasant bread eaten and stolen is sweet. Pleasant bread eaten in secret is sweet. Stolen waters are sweet. Go the way of the world. Climb the ladder of success the world's way. Step on whoever you have to if it gets you to the top. Have an adulterous affair. Who cares? Live your own life and if it feels good, do it." However, we have godly wisdom crying out saying, "Learn of Me. Find Me. I will give you life, health, strength, joy, and peace." The way of folly is easy to choose. Sometimes the harder road is to pursue the Wisdom of God, but in the end one winds up in the grave of hell and the other ends with eternal life seated in heavenly places.

Through the work of the Cross, Christ has made wisdom available to us and given us the opportunity to choose. Every day we have the choice to live a life filled with godly wisdom or frivolous folly. If we are going to enjoy a life a good success, we are going to have to have the wisdom of God. Our five natural senses will have to begin to be led by the Holy Spirit and we are going to have to stop living according to our own desires and pleasures.

We must seek, and find, God's plan for our lives as it is revealed by the Holy Spirit. Wisdom and mercy walk hand in hand. Even though we may have made wrong choices yesterday, we get another chance today. The Cross bought the abundant mercy of God, and we have the opportunity to choose.

When Adam and Eve chose the wrong tree, there was a guard set up with a sword so they could not even get to the Tree of Life. Yet because of the Cross, today if we choose the wrong fruit one day, we are still welcome back to the Tree of Life the next. That is God's mercy and grace. That is why wisdom is the beginning of the fear of the Lord. True understanding is to know God. May the wisdom of God come into our lives like never before. As believers, let's make the choice from this moment on to seek wisdom and begin to live a life of good success.

Stewardship

Stewardship: The conducting, supervising, or managing of something; *especially*: the careful and responsible management of something entrusted to one's care.
"We make a living by what we get; we make a life by what we give." — Winston Churchill

Chapter Nine

A large part of enjoying a life of Good Success in God is about stewardship. When we understand God's generous nature and His character, one of our first questions as believers should be, "What are we going to do with provision when God gives it to us?" What are we going to do when God does bless us and gives us good success?" Proverbs 3:27-28 cuts right to the chase, "Do not withhold good from those to whom it is due, when it is the power of your hand to do so. Do not say to your neighbor, go and come back and tomorrow I will give it, when you have it with you." In this portion of Proverbs Chapter Three, let's visit issues about money, time, possessions, homes, education, career, exercise, health, families, and wisdom. These are all things God has given us and are the tools in the Bible He means for us to utilize so that we can become a blessing to others.

The Purpose of Success

The purpose of living a life filled with success is that we have the ability and power to help others. In Genesis 12:2 God told Abraham, "I will bless you and make you a blessing." The reason God blessed Abraham in such a powerful way was because He wanted him to be a blessing to the nation of Israelites that God was about to give birth to. God blesses us so that we may become a beacon of hope to our communities, state, nation, and literally the nations of the world. There will come a day, if we trust God and believe Him, that nations will come and we will lend to them and not borrow. There is going to come a day when nations are going to be fed from the abundance God has blessed His people with.

Being successful for the sake of being successful is a world system mind set and has no impact on the Kingdom of God whatsoever. God wants us to be successful so we can help others. God wants us to enjoy good success so we can share our experience and begin to multiply, thereby increasing the Kingdom. Actually, Matthew 10:8 directs us to walk in the revelation that "freely you have received, freely you should give." As we begin to really live in this revelation and demonstrate God's power and plan, through giving, nations are going to be blessed.

A great example of how God will birth men and women to bless nations is Ulf Eckman. He was ministering in Russia and had a vision of a train. He saw the train going right through the old Soviet Union and he believed God had shown him a vision of how to reach that nation.

At first he perceived it to be a prophetic vision of God sending His Spirit, like a train, through that nation. However, God had something entirely different planned. Ulf's associate, Karl Gustoff, was in the nation at the time and the KGB were following him around. God instructed him to ask the KGB agent assigned to him if he wanted to come to Sweden for an all expense paid vacation. Being the KGB and a citizen of the Soviet Union, and never having been out of Russia, he took him up on the offer and went to Sweden

When he went there, he was blessed. He went to their church and saw what they were doing. He approached Ulf and asked "How would you like to have a train?" He said, "What do you mean?" He asked again, "How would you like to have a train that runs the entire length of the Soviet Union?"

Ulf had what he thought was a prophetic vision two years before. He asked again, "What do you mean?" The man responded with, "A real train, that goes from one side to the other of Russia that they used to teach Marxism. Would you like to have it and use it? For one hundred dollars I will get you a train."

For one hundred dollars they had access to a train that went from one side of Russia to the other. They filled it with Bible students, Bibles and headed out across the Soviet Union. At every stop they preached and planted churches. Now there are hundreds of churches planted in the Soviet Union because of a Holy Spirit inspired train ride through the old Soviet Union. God used that unlikely association to bless an entire nation.

Ulf did it because God provided him with the resources and he had it in the power of his hand to do. He could have said, "We are happy in Sweden. We are blessed, we have a great congregation, but he knew God had provided a way for him to evangelize the entire nation of Russia.

When it is in the power of our hands to do it, we have to be obedient to what God is asking of us. Expanding the Kingdom has never been, nor will it ever be, about Christians being blessed, building a structure, raising a strong congregation and sitting (or standing) in said structure singing about how blessed they are.

Do Something for Somebody

God is raising up people who want to do something for somebody. People say, "I do not feel led." It is time to get the lead out and do something. Good success is about being faithful with the small measure of success that we begin with so God can increase that small amount from little to much so that we are enjoying good success for our lifetime.

In the end, the only thing that is really going to matter is what we do for eternity. Luke 12:16-21 makes a very powerful case about this, "Then He spoke a parable to them, saying: 'The ground of a certain rich man yielded plentifully.' And he thought within himself, saying, 'What shall I do, since I have no room to store my crops?' So he said, 'I will do this: I will pull down my barns and build greater, and there I will store all my crops and my goods. And I will say to my soul, "Soul, you have many goods laid up for many years; take your ease, eat, drink, and be merry. "' But God said to him, 'Fool! This night your soul will be required of you; then whose will those things be which you have provided?' So is he who lays up treasure for himself, and is not rich toward God."

The old saying that a hearse never goes down the street with a U-Haul behind it is true. We are not going to take anything with us, and at the end of the day, what is going to matter is when we stand before God and answer the question of what we did with what He gave us.

What we accomplish for the Kingdom of God is all that will matter. In Matthew 6:33 we are encouraged to understand this revelation, "But seek the Kingdom of God, and all these things shall be added to you." At some point Christians have gotten it backwards, especially in our charismatic circles. We have started seeking *things* instead of the Kingdom. God said seek the Kingdom *first* and *then* things will be added to us. When we purpose in our hearts to be a blessing to the Kingdom of God and to His people, He will begin to pour His promises through our lives to make us a blessing.

Luke 12:32-35 gives us guidelines to follow, "Do not fear, little flock, for it is your Father's good pleasure to give you the Kingdom. So sell what you have, and give alms; provide yourselves money bags which do not grow old, a treasure in the heavens that neither does not fail, where no thief approaches, nor moth destroy. For where your treasure is, there your heart will be also." God encourages us to "Lay up treasures that are really going to count for eternity." Let's begin to think about heavenly principles when we think about success and what God wants us to do. The only thing that is going to matter at the end of the day is what happens for eternity.

What the Kingdom of God is Like

Matthew 25:14-30 states, "For the kingdom of heaven is like a man traveling to a far country, who called his own servants and delivered his goods to them. And to one he gave five talents, to another two, and to another one, to each according to his own ability; and immediately he went on a journey. Then he who had received the five talents went and traded with them, and made another five talents. And likewise he who had received two gained two more also. But he who had received one went and dug in the ground, and hid his lord's money. After a long time the lord of those servants came and settled accounts with them. So he who had received five talents came and brought five other talents, saying, 'Lord, you delivered to me five talents; look, I have gained five more talents besides them.' His lord said to him, 'Well done, good and faithful servant; you were faithful over a few things, I will make you ruler over many things. Enter into the joy of your lord.' He also who had received two talents came and said, 'Lord you delivered to me two talents; look, I have gained two more talents besides them.' His lord said to him, 'Well done, good and faithful servant; you have been faithful over a few things, I will make you ruler over many things. Enter into the joy of your lord.' Then, he who had received the one talent came and said, 'Lord I knew you to be a hard man, reaping where you have not sown, and gathering where you have not scattered seed. And I was afraid, and went and hid your talent in the ground. Look, there you have what is yours.' But his lord answered and said to him, 'You wicked and lazy servant, you knew that I reap where I have not sown, and gather where I have not scattered seed. So, you ought to have deposited my money with the bankers, and at my coming, I would have received back my own with interest. Therefore, take the talent from him, and give it to him who has ten talents. For to everyone who has, more will be given, and he will have abundance; but from him who does not have, even what he has will be taken away. And cast the unprofitable servant into the outer darkness. There will be weeping and gnashing of teeth."

That is a frightening Scripture because we can clearly see the opportunity that God gave to each individual and what the results are when we don't make the most of our spiritual and natural gifts. The part of the Scripture that says the offender will be cast out into outer darkness does not necessarily mean hell or loss of salvation. The connotation is *regret based*. It *would be* hell to live eternally knowing we could have done far more with what we had for the Kingdom while we were on the earth.

The gifts in the parable of the talents are money, time, possessions, family, or education. The parable is about what we have been given to use for the Kingdom of God. Even our own health is a contributing factor in how we share our gifts. The Bible acknowledges our bodies are the temple of the Holy Spirit and we are accountable for how we treat them. God wants us to stay healthy so we can do great exploits for the Kingdom.

When we begin to look at the talents in verse fourteen, we see the property owner delivered his goods to them, "For the Kingdom of heaven is like a man traveling to a far country that called his own servants and delivered his goods to them." From this Scripture we determine that what we have is not our own. What we have belongs to God. In Psalm 24:1 we observe, "The earth is the Lord's and all its fullness and the world and those who dwell in it." What we do have is to benefit the Kingdom of God. Verse 14 continues, "For the kingdom of heaven is like a man traveling...." John 15:16 says, "You did not choose Me, but I chose you and ordained you that you might go and bear fruit and that your fruit might remain." I Peter 2:9 states, "We have been translated out of the kingdom of darkness into the Kingdom of light."

It is not our responsibility to be successful as the world perceives success and to build the kingdoms of this world. It is our responsibility to build the Kingdom of God and see it established in the earth. I once heard a man say something so powerful. He said, "I would rather fail at a cause that will ultimately succeed, than to succeed at a cause that ultimately will fail." Ultimately, the Kingdom of God is the only Kingdom that is not going to be shaken.

God never asks more from us than we can handle. Matthew 25:15 makes that clear, "And to one he gave five talents, to another two, to another one and to each according to his own ability and immediately he went on a journey." He divided the talents in proportion to their ability. We cannot complain about having too little because if we put it in the hands of God, He will make it much. Many people who never do anything for the Kingdom of God say they do not have the education, money, time, or enough of this or enough of that, but if we will start using the little that we do have, God will turn it into much. If we are not using the little we have now for God, we will not use any increase for Him either.

Follow Biblical Examples

The key is to start with what we do have and begin to follow biblical examples. How about the woman who gave her last meal? How about the widow's mite? How about the little boy's lunch of two loaves and five fish? How about Gideon's three hundred? How about Jesus' twelve? Jesus had twelve disciples and shook the world with them. They depended on God and they did not wait to see what God was going to do for them. They began to exercise the gifts and talents they did have, and the ones they did not have, God provided for them.

We may never accomplish anything for the Kingdom if we wait until we get something. If we wait until we become educated, trained, or receive money, we may be waiting until Jesus comes back and be found like the unprofitable servant who did nothing with what God had given him.

I once met a powerful man of God in Zimbabwe named Dr. Goody. He has preached there for forty years. The first twenty plus years he rode a bicycle from village to village. That was his only mode of transportation as he traveled around Zimbabwe. He rode a bicycle to plant churches and further the Kingdom. He rode for miles in the heat of Africa to plant churches, and he now has *four thousand churches*.

He has many spiritual gifts, but he had a *revelation* of developing others gifts and talents. He started teaching his church to use whatever talent they had for God. He encouraged them to use every talent, no matter how great or small, for the Kingdom and to not expend it on self or career. He taught them to utilize their gifts outside of what they did to make money and use it for God. His congregation was taught and trained that regardless of what it was, making baskets or cleaning yards, to take that talent and the money received for the effort and give it to the Kingdom.

The ladies' ministry really caught the principle. They started weaving baskets, selling them, and giving the money to the Kingdom. God started blessing them so much that they started selling them on the streets. They became so successful that they built a factory that manufactures baskets, and all of the proceeds continue to expand the growth of the Kingdom of God in that region of Africa today.

When I was there these women had prospered to the degree that they were able to buy Dr. Goody a beautiful new car. They took the little they had and God made it much. I rode to a crusade in his car and it was a powerful experience to be with that humble man of God who had ridden a bicycle for all those years to build the Kingdom.

We were in the new car and the vent was blowing and we asked,

"Dr. Goody, why don't you turn the air on?" He answered, "The air is on." We said, "No, Dr. Goody that is the vent." We pushed that A/C button and cold air shot out. He shouted, "Hallelujah!" That humble man of God did not even know the A/C in the car was not on and did not care. He was happy to have wheels that he did not have to peddle.

We, especially as Charismatic Christians, have gotten so caught up with prosperity that we have seemingly forgotten about the Kingdom. Stop praying for a new car. When we start using the old car that we already have to pick someone up and take them to church, God will upgrade the cars we have. Pick someone up if you see them walking and bring them to church with you. Stop praying for a new home, and start using the home you have for the Kingdom. Once that one has been outgrown, God will give you another one. When we allow God to utilize the few talents we have, He will begin to multiply them into many.

What we have is ours to invest, work with, bury, or join with others to build the Kingdom. Whatever God has entrusted to us He wants us to use for His Kingdom. It is up to us what we do with it. Remember the servant who received five bags of gold, invested it, and doubled it? The servant with two bags of gold doubled it. The servant with one bag dug a hole and hid it. The Word tells us he was afraid and that may have been part of why he decided to hide his talent rather than invest his portion.

Fear does stop us from doing things at times. Fear will stop us from taking risks for the Kingdom of God, especially the fear of man. We all are afraid that we will make fools out of ourselves at some point in our lives. That fear has the potential to stop us from doing anything for God. Over the years, I have preached to thousands of people. Recently, I had the opportunity to preach to department heads at a local hospital.

Someone Needs to Hear

There were only to be forty in attendance, but I was losing sleep about speaking to this group of businessmen. Then I started thinking, "Well, why did I even accept the invitation? I do not have to go down there. But, and yes, there is always a but, in this type of situation, God said, "Yes, you do. Someone there needs to hear about the Kingdom of God."

I purposed to go and figured even if I did make a fool of myself, they would never see me again. My pep talk to myself went like this, "You go and say what God wants you to say and use the little bit that you have." I went thinking that God was not going to use my gift to accomplish much of anything, but afterward I was pleasantly surprised as people came and told me how much hearing the Word of God had impacted their life.

When we let God direct our paths, we get out there and are often way beyond our comfort zones. He increases our gifts and talents to be a blessing to those who really need to hear the Word of God. So many of us are bound by the fear of man that we let these amazing opportunities pass us by.

Sometimes it is fear, but more often than not it is pure selfishness. We would rather make sure our house is comfortable than going to make sure somebody else's house is comfortable. Truthfully, our culture lends itself to selfishness and we have become selfish people who are concerned with our four and no more. Many of us have so much of everything and so many others have so little.

My wife sold all of her antiques so I could go on my first ministry trip. She has always been ready to sacrifice for the Kingdom. After we started the church, God put a ministry on her heart to go to people's homes that needed to be improved or decorated. The ministry is aptly named Trading Graces. She started calling around and asking, "What do you have extra, a lamp, table or a bed?" The next question was, "How would you like to be part of a team that will change people's lives?"

What is so amazing is how much extra we do have. A couple of lamps out in storage, or a bed in the basement, an extra kitchen table, and an empty house will be partially furnished. We do not have to have a house full of furniture to give. An extra table, two lamps, a dining room, a couch here and a chair there, a rug here, and voilà, the transformation is complete. The next thing you know a house has become a home. At this point in time, we have literally lost count of the number of homes that have been refurbished and the people who have been blessed through the ministry God called a handful of women to who were not afraid to put their gifts to work.

We have to move past our place of security to taking a few risks. It is not a great risk to give away a chair that you aren't using. Here is the challenge: Give your good chair, not the one in the basement. Start doing things like that and God will start blessing you in powerful ways. Matthew 25:19 reminds us that what we do have counts to God, "After a long time, the lord of those servants came and settled accounts." This Scripture made me think of people who have served in the Kingdom of God, people who have faithfully sacrificed for the Kingdom of God, and have been rewarded in *this life*.

God provides for those who are faithful to use their gifts for Him. Recently, an older man went to be with the Lord and the story surrounding his life is a reminder of how faithful God is to those who have a heart after Him. This gentleman was faithful to share the gospel everywhere he traveled. One of the places he frequented was an auto repair shop where the men were less than receptive to his evangelistic efforts. Each time he would begin to share what God had done in his life, the men would mock and jeer at him. Yet he would appear in his road worn vehicle periodically and endeavor to share his love for Jesus. After he died, his vehicle was taken to the very same shop for repairs. Upon examination, a new mechanic declared that the car was beyond repair and determined that it must have been on blocks and out of commission for at least two years. Apparently, every component in it was rusted and corroded. He said there was no way that car ran.

The men in the shop were amazed. They knew the man had driven the same vehicle for years. The man *had* been driving it for years and had never done anything to it. After he died, the car would not even start, much less run. God is faithful to those who are faithful to Him.

Accounts are going to be settled and people who have given, sacrificed, and loved God will be on the receiving end of great rewards. Jesus is coming back for praying mothers, grandmothers, Sunday school workers, ushers, parking lot attendants, and givers. He is going to settle accounts for those who have sown into the Kingdom of God. The last are going to be first, and the first are going to be last. What we do with our talents in this life is going to determine what we have in the next life. To the degree that we are faithful here is the degree we are going to enjoy eternity. We would like to believe everything is going to be equal in heaven. However, that is not the case and further good news is that we are not going to stay in heaven. We are only going to be there for a celebratory meal.

A New Heaven and Earth

God is going to make a new heaven and a new earth. We are not going to live in heaven. When the new earth manifests, those who were faithful on earth are going to rule. All we are going through here is training for reigning. We are going to rule with the Lord when He comes back.

We have this Christian mentality that we are going to sit in heaven, play harps and wear diapers. In reality we are coming back for a new heaven and a new earth, and we are going to live eternally, ruling and reigning in this new world.

We have to continually think like that when we are giving, working, and when we are being stretched. We have to live in the revelation that one day whatever we do in this life is going to count in that life. It changes our whole perspective of life on earth and what our goals are when we understand that whatever we do here is going to mean something there, and we are going to be rewarded for it.

Rick Joyner, who is a true prophetic voice in the earth today, had a powerful vision. This is a two-part vision and the first half of it occurred in the natural realm. He was sitting in a park one day and was not living out the plans and purposes of the Kingdom. He saw an old drunk who was a street person, walking across the street with a wine bottle in his hand. As the story goes, a cat jumped right in front of the old drunk. He looked at the cat and was about to kick it as hard as he could. Right before he let go with a kick that would have surely put an end to the cat he said, "Um," left the cat and walked on by. That actually happened and Rick witnessed it.

A couple of years later, he had a vision of heaven and he was in the throne room of God. Around the throne there were people worshipping God, but the line went way away from the throne. In the vision, he was in the throne room but was far away from the throne.

As he looked around he began to recognize preachers and teachers of the Word that he honored very highly. He was surprised as he saw them and he asked, "What are you doing so far back here from the throne?" And they answered, "Oh, this is our place." And he asked, "What do you mean?" The answer was, "Well, it is hard to explain. We are all happy here; we are all glad we are here, but some of us are closer to God here than others." Rick asked, "What do you mean?" He said, "To the degree we used what God gave us is the degree that we get to experience God here." He said, "Yes, but you were one of the greatest teachers. I learned so much from the revelation you had and the things you poured into my life." He said, "Yes, that is true, but most of my reward I got down there via adulation, praise, and achievements." He said, "You know what? When I got here I realized that I had only used about a fraction of what God had given me."

In the vision Rick talked to all these different men, and as he talked he kept moving closer to the throne of grace. He got right next to the throne and what he saw amazed him even further. There, right at the throne, was the drunk that had not kicked the cat. He said, "My God, this cannot be right. God," he said, "That great teacher of the Word of God is at the back and that guy that I saw with that cat is here." God said these words, "He took every measure of grace that he had been afforded to not kick that cat. The man you saw at the back had multitudes of grace that he never used." Rick came out of that vision with a whole new perspective of what heaven is going to be like.

There are going to be people there that we thought would not even get in. Heaven is going to be totally different than what we ever thought or imagined. When we minister to people, we never know what is going to happen and who we are going to touch and to what degree grace will be given to overcome circumstances and situations. Our prayer should be, "God let me use every ounce of grace I have today."

We have not all been afforded the same grace. Some of us have much more than others. The wonderful aspect of God's character that evens this all out is that what will be required is what we have, not what we do not have. All that is going to matter on that day is what we did with what we had. What we do with our talents in this life is going to determine what rewards we have in the next.

When We are Faithful

When we are faithful with what we do have, more is going to be given. If we will be faithful in the little, God will give us more. When my wife and I first started in ministry, everywhere we went I preached the same sermon. God gave me a sermon entitled, "Suddenly." Boy, did I preach that sermon. Bev would ask, "What are you preaching tonight?" I would answer, "Suddenly." "What are you going to preach in the morning?" "Suddenly." She would say, "That is what you preached tonight." I would tell her, "I am going to say it differently." That is the only sermon I had. What was so encouraging was that each time I preached it, God would move powerfully. Until He gave me something else to say, I preached what I had.

During this time I owned two suits, a blue one and a gray one. One night I would wear blue, one day gray, the next blue and gray, and the next gray and blue. We were using what we had to get started. Our office was two popcorn tins with a telephone and an answering machine, but we used what we had to get started.

All I had in the very beginning was my testimony. Revelation 12:11 encourages us that we overcome by the Blood of the Lamb and the word of our testimony. If He had never given me any other revelation and it meant that every time I stood up to preach that I tell my testimony, I will be able to answer God when on that day He asks, "What did you do with what I gave?" I will be able to say I gave my testimony everywhere I went God. I have told my testimony. It may be the only thing we have, but as we are faithful to share it God will give us more revelation and a deeper understanding of His purpose and plan in the Kingdom.

Share your testimony, preach the sermon that you have, pray with whatever power you do have, and God will honor your effort. Start praying for little things, then God will answer when you pray for bigger things. It would seem that the problem is we are always talking about what we do not have instead of utilizing what we do.

I was so impressed one day when I was in England. I was about to preach and was going to share my testimony. I asked God, "Can I do something other than talk about my testimony?" I opened up the book of Acts and this word jumped out at me. Paul said, "I must testify in Rome." I said, "I must testify in London, Paul." Paul was a very wise man, but he was not that eloquent of a man. He said, "I did not come to you in eloquence of speech. I came to you in the power and demonstration of the Holy Spirit. " He would testify about what God had done for him and God would use him very powerfully. When we take the little we have, and use it to further the Kingdom, God will give us more.

The master said of the one who had hidden his talent, "Take his away and give it to the man who had ten." He that has will have more and he that has not, even that which he has will be taken away. God is saying that the gifts and talents that lie dormant too long are going to be given to someone else that can be trusted with them. When we do not use our talents for God, He will ultimately activate them in someone who will use them to build the Body of Christ and the Kingdom.

John 10:10 is an interesting portion of Scripture. "The thief does not come except to steal, to kill, and to destroy. I have come that they may have life, and that they may have *it* more abundantly." It is interesting because it has been taught that Satan is the thief. In reality it is a warning about false teaching and false shepherds. Anything we have lost is either because it became a distraction, God removed it, or because we were not good stewards. God gave our gifts to us and they are without repentance. That means He does not take them back, but He will redistribute them. God will give us every opportunity to be good stewards, and the thing that we lose is the benefits when we do not share our spiritual and natural gifts with others.

We do not have to wander around worrying about the devil stealing our good success. All we have to do is be good stewards of what God gives us. The man in this passage of Scripture was not called wicked because he failed; he was wicked because he did not try. He did not try to expand or build upon what God gave him.

Bev and I have a policy: Whatever passes through our hands, we want it to leave in better shape than it arrived in. If it is clothing, cars, tools, or a home, whatever it is, we want it leave in better condition when it passes through our hands.

God wants every circumstance, situation, tribulation, and trial that comes through our life to leave us better than when it came. As we grow and mature, we have the capability to be continual conduits of God's healing flow for others. There have been many times that I have asked God what He wanted me to be in the Kingdom. Was I a Pastor, Prophet, an Apostle or perhaps an Evangelist? God finally answered through a man of God while we were ministering in Iceland. He prophesied and answered my question. He told me that God has called me to be a pipe. I did not know that being a pipe was a fivefold ministry but that is what God said. He said, "I want you to be a pipe." You may ask what that means. Pipes are almost invisible. They run underground and behind walls and are not seen. Their function is to take the source to the need. To be a pipe for God we take the source to the need.

Once, while traveling in New York City, I had the opportunity meet Mother Teresa. What a frail, little woman she was. She was walking along addressing every person she met. In each hand she placed a little coin and stuck her own hand out as she said these words, "When you open your hand to do something, remember this, you did it unto Him." 1).You 2). did 3). it 4). unto 5). Him.

I looked at this tiny, wizened, bent over woman and thought, "My God, what she has accomplished for the Kingdom of God." She understood that when she did something for someone else, she did it for Him. It did not matter if it was for one or one thousand, she knew she was doing it for the Lord.

In Calcutta I saw the devastating poverty that a handful of missionaries are trying to overcome. At the helm of the mission we were visiting was Hilda Bontain, a missionary in Calcutta who feeds 20,000 people daily. We walked streets filled with every kind of heartbreak and tragedy you can imagine with the bodies of dead children and babies lining the streets.

Every morning a trash truck makes its way through the city streets and picks them up and throws them in the truck. It is an unbelievable atmosphere to work in. As we viewed the desolation, she looked at our team and said, "If somebody will hold the rope, I will go to the pit. I just need somebody to hold the rope." That kind of dedication touches your heart so powerfully. If they can do so much with the little that they have to reach so many, what can we do with what we have for the Kingdom of God?

When we give of what we have we may never know how many lives it actually impacts. God knows where our gifts and talents will be best utilized, and the best direction for us to follow is to leave judgment, pride, envy, and strife behind. We have to proceed at times with caution and not be so quick to pass by those who may not look like somebody we would want to socialize or fellowship with. In Matthew 25: 40 Jesus said, "When you have done it to the least of these, My brethren, you have done it unto Me."

Matthew 6:19-21 teaches us to, "not lay up for yourselves treasures on earth, where moth and rust destroy and where thieves break in and steal, but lay up for yourselves treasures in heaven, where neither moth nor rust destroys and where thieves do not break in and steal. For where your treasure is, there your heart will be also." This Scripture reminded me of the movie *Schindler's List*. Oscar Schindler created jobs, sold possessions, and risked his own life to save Jews. At the end of the war he is questioned himself as to why he did not sell more, work harder, and do whatever it would have taken to have saved one more life. It could be *our* dollars that helps a mission team fulfill the mandate on their lives and saves the lives of others.

Giving money and blessing people will not cause us to inherit heaven. Heaven is our inheritance as heirs that came through the Blood of Christ. What we do for people will be laid up for our account, in heaven, when Jesus settles accounts. I want to stand there on that day and hear, "Well done My good and faithful servant." Some of us may never have won anything or stood before great people, had great praise or adulation or great reward. Imagine what it is going to be like that day to stand before millions of people and hear the Lord say, "Well done My good and my faithful servant." Some of us have been given a lot. Some of us have been given a little. The good news is that all we are required to do is to do something with the increment we have. Some of us have a lot of money, time, health, strength, education, a great career, a beautiful home, and a wonderful family. Many of us have none of the above, and then there are those who are somewhere in the middle. The question remains, "What are we going to do with what we have?"

Have You Shown Any Interest?

Not long ago I saw a sign on a church marquee that floored me. It said, "God gave Christ to invest in you. Have you shown any interest?" It does not matter how rich, poor, or educated we are, ultimately, the question we are going to answer, as believers, is what did we do with the gifts God gave us? All that is going to matter on that day is what we did for Jesus and what we did with everything we have been given.

It is really a joy to be good stewards and it truly is more blessed to give than receive. The littlest things can mean so much. As believers it is important that we mature in Christ-likeness and begin to look for every opportunity to do something for Him and His people. It does not matter how small or insignificant it may seem.

Our daily prayer should be, "God give me the opportunity to be a blessing to someone today." If at the end of the day all we are working for is "good success" for our four and no more, then we are on the wrong path and need to go in the opposite direction. Paul said, "If we only believe in this life, we are men most miserable." We have an opportunity to build the Kingdom of God every day that we live in the world. Remember, "We make a living by what we get; we make a life by what we give." —Winston Churchill

Soul Ties

Soul: The quality that arouses emotion and sentiment.
Tie: Something typically constituting a restraining power, influence.

Chapter 10

I don't like you, but I love you, Seems I'm always, thinking of you, Oh, you treat me badly, I love you madly, You really got a hold on me, Baby, I don't want you, but I need you, Don't wanna kiss you, but I need you, you do me wrong now, My love is strong now, Baby, I love you and I want you, just hold me, Don't want to leave you, Don't want to stay here, Don't want to spend, another day here, You really got a hold on me. –Smokey Robinson-

Remember that old Smokey Robinson song *You Really Got a Hold on Me?* Or how about *All Tied Up* by CoCo Lee, "I can't think, and I can't eat, It's three in the morning, and I can't even sleep, Cuz I'm all tied up in you, and I don't know what to do, Sometimes I can't think, sometimes I can't speak, it's a crying shame, what you've done to me, Cuz I'm all tied up in you,. I'm so all tied up in you. " These two artists may not realize it, but they are demonstrating symptoms of classic soul tie relationships.

In the 21st century God is speaking to the Body of Christ about the issue of soul ties and how to be delivered from ungodly relationships that have bound His people. Often, ungodly soul ties deceive and damage us. These ungodly ties have the power and potential to destroy the plans and purposes of God for our lives. Relationships from our past may still be affecting our present and keeping us from living in the fullness of God's blessings. Or soul ties that we do not even recognize may be controlling our present, preventing us from moving into all that God has for us.

Godly Soul Ties

An example of a godly soul tie is found in the description of Jonathan and David's relationship in I Samuel 18:1-4, "Now when he had finished speaking to Saul, the soul of Jonathan was knit to the soul of David and Jonathan loved him like his own soul. Saul took him (David) that day and would not let him go home to his father's house anymore. Then Jonathan and David made a covenant because he loved him as his own soul. And Jonathan took off the robe that was on him, and gave it to David, and stripped himself of his armor, even to his sword and bow and belt."

David and Jonathan were knit so tightly together that their souls became like one. Jonathan had a revelation that David was heir to the throne and because of the love that God gave them for one another as brothers he gave him his robe, which represented his position in his father's house. He willingly gave his armor, his position in the army, and his rights as heir to the throne to David. This kind of love and soul tie is scriptural. John 15:3 tells us, "No greater love does a man have for his friend than to lay his life down." That, in fact, is a godly soul tie.

Marriage is also a godly soul tie. We should be tied to our wife or husband by a covenant soul tie. Marriage should be one of the strongest, godly soul ties we have. In Matthew 19:5 the Pharisees ask Jesus about marriage. He answered them and said, "A man shall leave his mother and father, and cleave to his wife, and the two of them shall become one."

They then began to ask Jesus about divorce. They reminded Him Moses had made provision for divorce. Jesus said, "Yes, he did, but he made provision because of the hardness of your hearts." He said from the beginning it was not to be like that, two were to become one and stay that way. To be equally yoked two must truly become one, not only with one another, but with Jesus as the third cord in the relationship. It is, of course, God's plan for every knee to bow to Christ as Lord, but according to I Corinthians 7:14 the believing husband or wife does sanctify the unbelieving spouse, and the relationship is clean before God. If the unbeliever believes and becomes part of the Kingdom, he begins to walk in the blessings and inheritance of God. Therefore, the enemy's plans and soul ties are destroyed.

However, I Corinthians 7:15 goes on to state this, "If an unbeliever departs, let him (or her) depart; a brother or a sister is not under bondage in such cases. But God has called us to peace." Furthermore, Matthew 5:31-32 is very specific about reasons for divorce to occur, "Whoever divorces his wife let him give her a certificate of divorce. But I say to you that whoever divorces his wife except for sexual immorality causes her to commit adultery; and whoever marries a woman who is divorced commits adultery." This limitation on divorce was instituted to protect the wife from being discarded for any reason other than immorality. According to Deuteronomy 24:1-4, a certificate of divorce was given if immorality was not involved, to *protect the wife's dowry* and to prevent unscrupulous husbands from taking advantage of faithful wives.

Divorce, in the times in which we live, is epidemic and is directly responsible for innumerable soul ties that have literally immobilized not only secular households but Christian families as well. In many denominations there is no restoration for a divorced person and absolutely no opportunity to fulfill ministerial destinies. Can divorce really be the worst and only transgression God will not forgive? Can it really be true there is no restoration for God's people after divorce?

2 Corinthians 5:17-19 demonstrates how our relationship with Christ affects every area of our lives. "Therefore, if anyone is in Christ, he is a new creation, old things have passed away; behold, all things have become new. Now all things are of God, who has reconciled us to Himself through Jesus Christ and has given us the ministry of reconciliation, that is, that God was in Christ reconciling the world to Himself, not imputing their trespasses to them and has committed to us the word of reconciliation. Now, we are ambassadors for Christ, as though God were pleading through us: we implore you on Christ's behalf, be reconciled to God. For He made Him who knew no sin to be sin for us, that we might become the righteousness of God in Him."

As ministers of reconciliation we should be imploring those bound by soul ties, broken by divorce, and beaten up by their own bad choices to, on Christ's behalf, be reconciled to God. Instead, countless thousands have been rejected instead of restored, and put out of the church never attaining the purpose God has for them. They have ended up right back in the world, justifying their actions and repeating the same pattern because they were not restored in church.

Revelation 3:19 tells us this, "As many as I love, I rebuke and chasten. Therefore be zealous and repent." This is not a license for lawlessness to divorce at the slightest whim. However, if every measure to be restored and reconciled has not broken through the hardness of heart of the person initiating the divorce, there is still life and ministry on the other side of divorce for believers through repentance and forgiveness.

The Sad Truth

The sad truth is many Christian marriages fail because of ungodly soul ties that were never dealt with before the marriage, and these issues slowly destroy relationships without individuals even realizing what caused the hard-hearted attitude in the first place.

Ungodly soul ties will harden our hearts toward the things of God. Soul ties will cause us to pervert sermons or Scriptures, make them fit our situation, and justify our soul ties making them acceptable. Instead of dealing with the problem by allowing God's truth and light to reveal dark and hidden secrets, we start taking Scriptures and try to make them fit our circumstance to make that secret thing inside of us all right.

In reality, it is not all right. We try to justify our behavior by perverting Scripture to give us an out in our situation. If we can in some way fit Scripture to our bondage, we then reason that it cannot really be bondage at all and even if we are bound, how bad can it really be if we have found a way to justify it? Truth, very likely, has been taught through the Word of God, but we have not recognized it as truth because it is filtered through a soul tie and the truth has become perverted. For us to truly walk in freedom and liberty, all ungodly soul ties must be destroyed from our lives.

There are Kingdom relationships in Christ that God will tie our hearts with that we will be willing to lay our lives down for. These are godly, covenant relationships that bring the blessings and promises of God.

An ungodly soul tie is just the opposite and will cause our soul to be tied to something outside of the will of God. It can be a person, relationship, place, thing, emotion, or an event that happened to us in our past during childhood our present as adults. It *can* be something that happened to us in our past but it is just as likely that that our soul is still tied to something in our more immediate experience.

If not dealt with, these ungodly soul ties will cause us to relinquish our rights as a believer. They will cause us to abort the plans and purposes God has for us. We can literally be disrobed and stripped of the God-given destiny He has for our lives as a result of holding onto ungodly soul-ties. That is why we need to cut soul ties from our lives once and for all. If this is new information, the question may be, how do soul ties begin? The ones previously listed are a few I have experienced personally. As this revelation begins to manifest in our minds and spirits, the Holy Spirit will reveal to us what particular situations and circumstances have held us in captivity and prevented us from receiving all God has for us.

God Wants Us to Have Good Success

3 John 1-3 begins with great exhortation, "The Elder, to the beloved Gaius, whom I loved in truth: Beloved, I pray that you may prosper in all things and be in health, just as your soul prospers. For I rejoiced greatly when brothers came and testified of the truth that is in you, just as you walk in the truth. I have no greater joy than to hear that my children walk in truth." It is exciting when we finally understand that God *wants* us to prosper. However, the degree to which we will prosper, materially, is in direct proportion to our souls prospering.

God wants us to have good success, but not to the point that it is above our capacity to handle. He has to do some work on our souls to enlarge our capacities to embrace the promises He has for us. When we become followers of Christ our *spirit* is instantly transformed and renewed by the Holy Spirit, but it is in the *realm of the soul* that the ongoing process of being transformed into the image of Christ takes place.

As Christians we have ignored the soulish realm when in reality that is where the real transformation happens. It is in that transformation that life or death, blessings or curses, come. Moreover, it is our eternal soul that matters. We will have eternal life in heaven because our spirit has been illuminated by God's plan and purpose, but we will not enjoy life, and life more abundantly on earth, if our souls remain bound.

We will never enjoy the maximum capacity of success that God has for us if we have not allowed God to transform our souls. Our heavenly Father cares just as much about our emotions and will as He does our spirits. That is why He wishes above all things that we be sanctified body, soul, and spirit. Salvation is not just about our spirit, it is also about our souls being in proper position to enjoy the fullness of life God has planned for us.

Many Christians live their lives on earth filled with guilt, condemnation, fear, doubt, unbelief, and all sorts of things that bind them up. They never enjoy good success or the blessings of God. The revelation that God cares about our souls and wants us delivered and free has in many ways languished on the back burner of collective theological principles. The question on the table is, how does our soul become liberated? The answer is found in John 8:32. It is because we walk in truth. Truth is the only thing that will set us free. "I am glad to hear that you walk in truth, I rejoice greatly when brethren came and testified of the truth that is in you, and I have no greater joy than to hear that my children walk in truth."

The Truth You Know Shall Make You Free

"You shall know the truth and the truth *you know* shall make you free." John 8:32 is all about the truth we *know*. For years I mistakenly thought that it is *truth* that sets us free, when in fact, it does not. It is the truth we *know* that sets us free. God's people perish from lack of knowledge because we have counted on someone else's revelation of the Word instead of seeking the truth of God's Word for ourselves. If we do not know the truth, it has no power to set us free. God wants to reveal His truth about our souls to us as individuals. *That* is what sets us free.

The only power the enemy has is deception. On Calvary's Cross, Satan's power was broken—his rule, authority, and dominion were destroyed. It is very clear that the enemy has been defeated when in Revelation 1:18 Jesus proclaims, "I Am He Who lives, Who was dead and behold, I am alive for evermore and I have the keys of hell and death."

The only power Satan has is found in Ephesians 4:14, "We should no longer be children, tossed to and fro and carried about with every wind of doctrine, by the trickery of men, in the cunning craftiness of deceitful plotting." The only power the enemy has is the power to deceive us. The only real tool he has in his arsenal is the ability to keep us bound by compelling us to keep secrets.

Secret Sins

Secret sins, faults, and addictions keep us in fear that someone will find out what we have worked so diligently to hide. For too long the church has been a place of judgment instead of a throne of grace. We have been afraid of being open and honest, and we live lives that are bound by the fear that someone will find out we are not perfect. Let's put that myth to rest right now. There is One Who is perfect and it is not us. So many people come to church, become followers of Christ, then because there is no mercy demonstrated, only a list of rules given, they go right back out into the world system and continue to live according to their five senses and the dictates of culture. The desire to do what God has called them to do may begin to manifest in their lives, but by that time that desire has been displaced by deception that they will never be accepted in a church. That strategy has proven to be very effective in delaying God's promise and process but it is not the final answer

People believe they cannot share their deepest secrets because of what Christians will think of them, so they keep living in the world system, still enslaved by culture and get sucked right back into sin because of soul ties in their lives. Secrets keep them bound because they have never been in an atmosphere of grace to be delivered from unnatural attachments that have become secrets in their lives that must be kept hidden at all cost. They may keep coming to church on Sunday but they are living in hell the rest of the week.

Every weakness represented in the human race comes to church, right along with the believer who has it, every week. Before we could even consider judging whoever is beside us, in front of us, or behind us, we must consider our own shortcomings and weaknesses. While we are trying to get the toothpick out of our brother's eye, let's be careful not to knock him in the head with the 2 x 4 that is in our own.

We have to realize there is an atmosphere of grace God has extended to His children and begin to live in it. God's grace allows us to tell the truth and ultimately be free. Matthew 12:29 puts it this way, if we can bind the strong man, we can spoil his goods. The enemy's number one desire is to bind (prevent God's purpose for our lives from being fulfilled) our souls so that he can enter in and spoil the goods God has blessed us with. He is a destiny and purpose thief. The enemy wants to divert our direction and keep us off track. Our destination is still heaven and our eternities are secure, but we will arrive not having fulfilled our purposes or destinies because we have not allowed the truth of God's mercy and grace to operate in our souls.

Sexual Immorality

I Corinthians 6:12-18 thoroughly addresses one of the strongest soul ties that men and women, through the generations, have dealt with. Paul said, "All things are lawful for me, but all things are not helpful. All things are lawful for me, but I will not be brought under the power of any. Food for the stomach, the stomach for food, God will destroy both it, and them. Now the body is not for sexual immorality, but for the Lord, and the Lord for the body. God both raised up the Lord, and will also raise us up by His power. Do you not know that your bodies are members of Christ? Shall I then take the members of Christ and make them members of a harlot, certainly not? Or do you not know that he who is joined to a harlot is one body with her, for two shall become one. But he who is joined to the Lord is one spirit. Flee sexual immorality. Every sin that a man does is outside the body, but he who commits sexual immorality sins against his own body."

Sexual sin joins us as one, and when the union of sexual intimacy takes place outside of the marital covenant, it becomes a sin against our own body. That is a soul tie. Why is the enemy so determined to cause people to fall into sexual immorality? If he is successful in perverting covenant relationships, a strong soul tie will be developed that will strip individuals of the plans and purposes of God.

When I was growing up I was told to not have sex outside of marriage, but no one ever told me *why*. It was just wrong. There was never an explanation of what happens spiritually when we become intimate without the covenant of marriage. The Word makes it clear that the two will become one. The *key is there has to be knowledge* of the Word to understand the ramifications of sin. Remember, it is the truth *we know* that sets us free.

What is often not understood is that when we join ourselves to a sexual partner outside of the will of God, we become one. What does that mean? It means we are joined not only in the sexual act, but also to every person they have had sex with. We have opened ourselves to generational curses and soul ties that are manifesting in our unsanctified sexual partners. Sexual immorality harms our bodies, emotions, spirits, and souls.

Satan's Strategy

It is imperative that we teach our children why it is wrong to engage in sexual immorality. There are physical consequences such as unplanned pregnancies and sexually transmitted diseases, but there are also spiritual consequences that are called *soul ties*. Once we have engaged in immoral behavior, those consequences have the potential to affect us for the rest of our lives if not dealt with. I dare say that most people I counsel with sexual problems have a soul tie to some relationship outside of the covenant of God, either in their past or present. Satan's strategy is to destroy each of us in our formative years with seeds of sexual immorality that can come through child abuse, pornography, or peer pressure to do something we are uncomfortable with. Later, it may start from loneliness or an unsatisfying marriage, and eventually end in sexual immorality.

It has been scientifically proven that pictures are so powerful that that what comes into our minds is stored there, *permanently*. That is why we have to be so careful about what we see and entertain with our eyes, because our brain stores visual input permanently.

I travel quite a bit and have spent a lot of time in Europe. I am a channel surfer and when I am tired and trying to relax, I just ride the channels. I do not really watch anything, I just surf. I learned early on that you have to be very careful in that part of the world because pornography is a regular part of their daily programming. Right in the middle of all the American game shows, movies, and European programming, bam, a pornographic scene will assault your senses.

Not surprisingly, it is not the *Price is Right* that stays in my mind's eye. I do not have problems going to sleep at night thinking about Drew Carey. Pornography, on the other hand is another story all together. Just an instant of it will plant itself there and we have to fight to get that image out of our minds, casting down every imagination that exalts itself above the name of Christ.

I do not choose to watch pornography, but in a moment's time I have the potential to see something that, as a visual, is now retained to memory. Because of the grace of God, I have such an intimate and open relationship with my wife that on the very few occasions I have had the experience just described, I immediately told my wife what had happened and came into agreement with her to cast down every imagination that would try to exalt itself above the name of Christ Jesus. That is where the rub is. Unfortunately, most of us do not have an atmosphere of grace at home, church, or in relationships in which we feel comfortable or safe enough to pick up the phone, call somebody, or go to someone and say, "Look, I was innocently surfing through the channels and this thought came to my mind, now it will not go away, please pray for me."

No Safe Zone

Because there is no safe zone to confess what happened, it becomes a secret. It is not yet a sin, but it is a secret. The enemy will then use that secret to develop a soul tie, and before we know it, we could be bound by pornography and cannot get away from it simply because we do not have an atmosphere of grace to ask someone to pray with and for us.

God created a mercy seat, and in these end times the church has to become a safe place for people to share intimate things in their lives so that they may begin to live freely for it is for freedom that we have been set free. There will no longer be judgment in the house of God, but rather a mercy seat where people can come and freely receive deliverance and not be the least bit concerned that another believer is going to judge them.

If God's mercy and grace does not begin to be demonstrated in churches, we will never be free. I live freely, enjoying my life and the grace the God has afforded me while I am here on the earth. I believe there is safety and security in openness and honesty. When we begin to live in transparency, the enemy cannot distract us with his tactics and mind games.

Samson was a mighty man of God with a great destiny ahead of him. He was used powerfully by God, yet the first recorded words that came out of Samson's mouth in Judges 14:1 were, "I saw a woman." He went down to Timna and said: "I saw a woman." Immediately, his weakness was out in the open. His weakness was exposed but it was never dealt with. He sought a wife who was not of his tribe because his eyes desired her. When that marriage did not work, he looked elsewhere and his eyes once again desired a woman.

Delilah was a prostitute but Samson loved her. She did everything within her power to discover the secret of his strength, but he would not tell her. In a moment of fleshly weakness he succumbed to her demands, and that was his ultimate demise. When he revealed his strength was to be found in his long hair, his destruction was imminent. She cut his hair and because of a soul tie, his mission, ministry, and manhood was destroyed. Samson was stripped of his God-given destiny. By God's grace his hair began to grow again. Even though we may be bald, spiritually speaking, and stripped of our God-given destiny, when we turn to God, and ask for deliverance from soul ties that are holding us back, our lives will begin to be restored. When Samson's hair began to grow back, it was the grace and mercy of God that allowed him to overcome and vanquish the very enemies who had been trying to slay him.

Bitterness and unforgiveness are also deadly weapons in the enemy's arsenal. A root of bitterness is like drinking poison and expecting someone else to die. Hebrews 12:15 warns, "Be careful lest a root of bitterness spring up in you and by that many be defiled." This portion of Scripture describes how Esau lost his birthright. Esau's problem was bitterness. He was jealous of his brother. Bitterness caused Esau to lose his birthright and the blessings of God that accompanied his inheritance. Even though he might not have gotten the blessing of the firstborn as was his right, God did have a plan for Esau's life.

At times, we as Christians, fight bitterness more than any other soul tie because bitterness is one of the enemy's most effective weapons to keep us from fulfilling our God-given destiny. It is amazing how unforgiveness and bitterness keep people who know the love, and forgiveness of God, bound.

I have counseled many men and women who are bitter toward people who have long since died. They allow a dead person to control their lives and destinies because of incidents in the past that are so painful it is as though they are still living the experience.

My wife and I experienced the healing power of forgiveness in our own lives. My wife's father was in prison for thirty-six years. My wife grew up in a very violent atmosphere and for many years dealt with a spirit of anger. When we first met she told me her natural father was dead. She did not even want to talk about him. At that time, she had not seen him for over sixteen years.

After salvation, we learned about the promises and blessings of God but we were not enjoying them. We struggled financially, spiritually, and physically. My wife battled one sickness after another. We lived from problem to problem. As we sought God, He revealed to her that she must go and release the bitterness in her heart by not only forgiving her father, but asking him to forgive her as well. *Many* of us have bitterness and unforgiveness that we keep putting Band-Aids on, but the wound is not healing and we are not getting better. The problem is not going away.

When we went to see her father she was determined to not only forgive him but to also ask his forgiveness. He was not very receptive to her that first visit, but that day *she* walked out of not only a natural prison but also a spiritual prison that had kept her bound for twenty-three years.

We drove away from the prison and out of nowhere a billboard appeared with these words painted on it: Do not give up, prayer works! We felt as if God put it there just for us. Two weeks later, we received a letter from the IRS forgiving us of a $100,000 debt. It was during the same time that we received phone calls with the exciting news that her three sisters and brother had all become followers of Christ. All of those blessings occurred within two weeks of her obedience to forgive her father. Because of soul ties to bitter emotions the whole family was being affected spiritually and held in captivity by a generational curse of anger. That is exactly what the devil does best. However, if we will get the issue, no matter what it is, out in the open, let the Holy Spirit intervene on our behalf, and through the Word of God cut that soul tie and release it to God, He will set us free.

The ultimate praise report for us is that when her father was released from prison he did come to live with us, and just as God had promised, he gave his life to the Lord shortly before his death. He may not have fulfilled all that God had for him, but he knew that he was forgiven, accepted, and loved.

Grief is another dehabilitating spirit that has the potential to wreak havoc in our lives. When not dealt with properly grief can take us to a place of bitterness. Through grief, if not careful, we can grow bitter toward God and be stripped of our God-given destiny. I once had a friend whom I traveled with in the ministry. In his former life he had been a heroin addict. He had been raised in a godly home and his father was a Pentecostal pastor, but he had lived in the world system for years. After many years of struggling with that addiction he went to church one night and said, "God, I love heroine more than I love You. If You will set me free I will serve You with all of my heart and life." The Spirit of God set him totally free and he was called into the ministry.

We traveled together for ten years. I slept in the same room with him more than I did with my wife. We traveled and worshipped God together all over the world. I knew the man inside and out. He loved God with all of his heart, but there were issues in his life he just could not overcome. His first grandchild was born with a birth defect and he could not understand how God would let something like that happen. At first he was angry, but then he began to grow bitter.

Because of bitterness he began to draw away from his wife. Darkness grew inside of him like poison. Instead of dealing with it and allowing God to heal him, he went back to what he knew would buffer his pain. Instead of going to God, he became enslaved to heroine, *again.* It was not an instantaneous downhill slide. It was a process. He had an addictive personality, so when he started developing old habits I knew he was heading down a road he should not be traveling. I reached out to him but he promised me he was alright. In the end it was a mercifully quick fall, fueled by his addiction that ended when he crashed and burned.

I flew home from preaching in Australia on New Year's Eve several years ago and received a phone call informing me he was in a hospital in New York City, dying. I flew there to be with him. By the time I arrived every organ in his body had shut down. I will never forget being in that hospital room with him. I grabbed his hand and lifted my hand and started singing one of the songs we used to sing. "The Lord is gracious and merciful. Full of kindness and good thoughts." I began to worship with him. I felt the Presence of the Lord minister to that broken man. Through tears I watched as he got his heart right with God. I said, "I promise you if you ask, God will heal you right now." He had tubes in every opening of his body and I asked, "Do you want me to pray for God to heal you?" He shook his head, "No." He had made his peace with God and was ready to go.

After he died and his family had said good-bye, I went back into the room and he had a giant smile on his face. I know he is with Jesus, but I believe with all of my heart it was premature because he allowed a soul tie to be resurrected that was rooted in anger, bitterness and grief. Because of bitterness and a soul tie to heroin, his God-given destiny was never fulfilled.

Sexual problems, bitterness, unforgiveness, grief, and fear are all emotions and actions that tie our souls to another person. Proverbs 25:29 tells us fear brings a snare. Fear knots and ties us up. Many people I meet are bound by fear. They are afraid of dying, sickness, failure, and man. They live in these fears all of their lives and never experience freedom.

I lived in the grip of fear for years. As a child, a spirit of fear had already attached itself to me when a home invasion absolutely terrorized me. Growing up in a small community in the sixties seemed very safe. Doors were left unlocked and at the age of eight it was not uncommon for me to get home from school before my mom arrived from work. On that particular day I got there before my sisters or my mom. Our house had been burglarized and fear gripped my heart. From that point on I could not sleep without the lights on. Because of fear I still wanted to sleep in the same room as my dad and mom long past the age of reason.

Fear kept me bound to the point that the maturation process got off track. It was always a part of my life. As I grew older I began to deal with it, but did not get delivered from it. For many people that is the problem: we learn to deal with our issues but do not get delivered from them. God does not want us to deal with soul ties; He wants us to be delivered from them.

I began to drink and do drugs, and my fears seemingly subsided. When I was high, I had no fears, so what did I do? I stayed high all of the time. For ten years of my life I was high every day because while I was high, I had no fear. I literally became addicted to the high that kept fear at bay. Little did I know that I had developed a soul tie to drugs because of fear. It was not my life's goal to become addicted to drugs, but it was the enemy's plan to trap me and prevent me from fulfilling what God had for me to do.

After I became a follower of Christ and was delivered from drug addiction, all of those fears came to the surface. I was a grown man and once again wanted to sleep with the lights and TV on all night. Each day new phobias and fears began to manifest until I thought I was going to lose my mind. I feared *everything*. With every little pain I thought I was going to die and that caused panic attacks. I battled all of these terrible fears and phobias until I realized I had a soul tie that needed to be destroyed by the Word of God. 2 Timothy 1: 7 assured me that God has not given me a spirit of fear, but of power, love, and a sound mind. I knew if I could renew my mind with the Word of God, I could be delivered.

Everywhere I went I listened to the Word. I often drove down the road terrified that I was not going to live to make it home, listening, listening, listening to the Word of God. At home I was just as frightened, but I continued to listen to, and learn, the Word. Eventually, I was freed from the spirit of fear. The Word of God is as powerful as a two edged sword and it will cut soul ties out of our lives.

Rejection and Insecurity

Rejection and insecurity are two other emotions that plague our lives. Fear births low self-esteem and insecurity and I was full of both emotions. When we develop low self-esteem, we begin to act out of insecurity. We become susceptible to peer pressure because we want to be accepted and fit in, when in reality it is a soul tie that needs to be cut from our lives. If not dealt with, we could spend the rest of our lives dealing with insecurity. Insecurity makes us believe that we are not good enough. That is why, if we really want to enjoy good success, we have to let God deal with these enemies of our soul.

Familiar Spirits

"Familiar spirits" are spirits that have attached themselves to our souls through familiar relationships and often through our family ties. They are better known as demonic spirits that are on assignment to pervert our family's destiny throughout the generations. These demonic entities manifest through curses that our grandparents and parents have had to deal with. Throughout family generations, familiar spirits attach themselves to our lives and wreak havoc if we allow them to continue.

What are generational curses? They are every manifestation that steals from us and prevents us from walking in the blessings of God. They are passed from generation to generation and run the gamut of destructive emotions and vices. Addiction, adultery, alcoholism, anger, divorce, depression, fear, rage, rejection, and all of the emotional issues that have been covered thus far are evidenced by soul ties. Exodus 34:7 explains how it happens, "God visits the third and fourth generations with the sins of the fathers."

Jesus spoke to three generations. He spoke to an adulterous generation, a perverse generation, and a chosen generation. By making the choice to live for the Kingdom of God we can come out of an adulterous generation. We can be free from a perverse generation and become part of a chosen generation who has been delivered out of the kingdom of darkness into His marvelous light. It should be our greatest desire to be part of this chosen generation.

Hebrews 4:12 gives us the weaponry necessary to cut soul ties: "The Word of God is living, powerful, sharper than any two-edged sword, piercing even the division of soul and spirit, and joints and marrow, and is a discerner of thoughts and intents of hearts, and there is no creature hidden from its sight." The Word of God is a two-edged sword and goes right to heart of our issues and reveals the problem. There is nothing hidden from the Word of God. It brings everything to light. If it only did that, it would be painful. If it only revealed the problem, it would not have the same power. Not only will the Word reveal what is there, it will cut it out and remove it. Not only will the Word reveal the problem, it will heal us.

A surgeon cuts to heal, not destroy. The Word is like that. Soul ties are like cancerous tumors in our body. They are an intrusion. They have nothing to do with us functioning or fulfilling our destinies. Yet if not detected they will become malignant and destroy us. God wants us to deal with these issues while they are benign. When we allow God to do the necessary surgery, not only does the Word cut them out, it destroys them.

God will begin to renew and restore our souls after His surgery, and then He will begin to renew and revive us. He will restore us through the Word of God so we will not think or act the way we used to. We will literally put off the old man and put on the new man because of the renewing power of God. Next, He will heal our bruises. Wounds are outward cuts or injuries. Bruises are inward injuries. Soul ties bruise people. It hurts inside where others cannot see. We may look great on the outside, but we are bruised on the inside. On the inside we have hurts, pain, soul ties and wounds that nobody knows about but us and God. All somebody has to do is touch on an unresolved issue and we react out of pain, do or say something in anger, or act in other ungodly ways. Those reactions happen when we have wounds we have not allowed God to heal.

Luke 4:18 states, "God is here to release those that are bruised and heal those that have been bruised." Isaiah 53: 5 is clear, "He was wounded for our transgressions and bruised for our iniquities." Jesus was bruised so that we might be healed. The teaching about the woman caught in adultery so touches my heart. Jesus forgave her and said, "Go, and sin no more." He did not say, "Go, and sin less" He said, "Go, and sin no more." Jesus wants to do a work so deep that we will not go back to what He has delivered us out of. When Jesus destroys that soul tie we will not go back to the lives we were living.

Be Separate

2 Corinthians 6:17 is a clarion call for God's people, "Come out from among them and be separate." That is why He calls us His Bride. God wants our souls tied to Him and not to anyone or anything else Matthew 22:37 describes what His desire is for us, "Love the Lord God with all your soul, mind, emotions, and will" He wants us to leave the world and cleave to Him. He does not want us contaminated by anything the world system has to offer. Jeremiah 3:1-5 asks, "If a man's wife left and had many lovers, wouldn't you consider her a polluted land and a defiled parcel? Wouldn't you consider her very unclean? God says you have had many other lovers, yet come back to me says God." We have allowed our souls to be tied to so many things other than God, but He wants to cut soul ties from these things and cause us to come out from among them and be separate. God desires for us to be free from anything that is preventing us from living in His promises and purposes. He wants His people free so that we can enjoy good success. Remember, "Beloved, I wish above all things that you prosper and be in health, even as your soul prospers."

His plan and desire is for us to be delivered and built up, growing stronger and stronger in Him while we are in the process of having our capacities enlarged. Nobody is completely free of temptation, but God does make a way of escape and our recovery time becomes much quicker. When I first became a follower of Christ and missed the mark, it sometimes took three or four months to recover. Then as I grew stronger, it would take three or four weeks. Thankfully, I am down to three or four minutes in most areas of my life. Not that I don't make mistakes, but I realize the enemy's strategies and I simply do not allow myself to be beaten up by fear, insecurity, low-self-esteem, or other forms of soul ties.

God wants us to be free in Him so that He can bless us. He wants to prosper us. "I know the thoughts and plans I have toward you, thoughts of a good success and expected end," says God. We will only enjoy that sort of life as our souls have the capacity to embrace and enjoy it.

Our heavenly Father does not want us to live our lives in bondage. He wants us to live in freedom. Regardless of the area in which we find ourselves trapped Isaiah 10:27 confirms, "The anointing will remove every burden and destroy every yoke." It is His desire that we live freely, delivered from soul ties and anything that encumbers us, so we can walk in the blessings of God, enjoying Good Success, God's Way, with a Lifetime Guarantee.

Kent Mattox is senior pastor of Word Alive International Outreach. He leads with passion and a strong vision to see people transformed by living a life of freedom in Jesus Christ. Kent has a gift of communication that allows him to present the gospel in a revelatory and refreshing manner. He teaches the Word with great insight and practical application. He lives with his family in Oxford, Alabama.